Meditation Vacations

Meditation Vacations

Guided Meditations for Relaxation & Healing

Amanda Jackson-Russell

* * *

Copyright © Amanda Jackson-Russell 2021.

The contents of this book (including the text and any illustrations and photographs, and the cover design, photographs and text) are the copyright of the author Amanda Jackson-Russell, in accordance with the Copyright, Designs and Patents Act 1988.

All rights reserved. No part of this publication may be reproduced, stored in a retrieval system, or transmitted in any form or by any means, electronic, mechanical, photocopying, recording or otherwise, without the prior written permission of the author, except in accordance with permissions stipulated in the Copyright, Designs and Patents Act 1988 (such as those related to use of extracts by educational establishments); in addition, scripts may be verbally recorded in audio form for personal (self-help) use only.

First published September 2021.
First edition September 2021.

Important Information, Disclaimers and Terms and Conditions of Use
~ When practising or considering practising any of the exercises in this book, you agree to assume responsibility for your own physical and mental wellbeing and you assume responsibility for any decision made regarding whether any particular practice is right for you.
~ Any information or exercises provided here are not an appropriate substitute for professional medical, psychological or psychiatric advice or care. You are advised to consult your medical practitioner before undertaking any alternative or complementary medical therapy or treatment or self-help programme.
~ The practices/scripts in this book cannot be taken as the recommendation of a medical practitioner, psychiatrist, psychologist, psychotherapist, hypnotherapist, or any other professional or alternative or complementary healthcare practitioner.
~ Practitioners who choose to use any of the material presented in this book with their clients take full responsibility for doing so.
~ Practitioners who employ the use of any of the scripts in this book agree to credit the author with the origin and copyright of any material used.
~ Any scripts or processes described herein that a reader verbally records in audio form will be employed for personal (self-help) use only.
~ Any unauthorised copying, reprinting or use of material in this book is prohibited.

Acknowledgements

I am grateful to so many wise and wonderful people who have helped to inspire my writing of these healing meditation scripts. Over the years, I have been privileged to study and/or work with individuals involved with the National Federation of Spiritual Healers (NFSH; now The Healing Trust), the British Wheel of Yoga (BWY), the Satyananda School of Yoga, Hay House, the College of Psychic Studies, and the Spiritualist Association of Great Britain, as well as a number of other organisations (for example, those involved in teaching Reiki and Hypnotherapy).

Much appreciation and gratitude is expressed, in particular, to Swami Dayamurti/Doriel Hall, Audrey Murr-Copland, the late Don Copland, Lilla Bek, Jane Garner, Stephanie Harrison (nee Collins), the late Philippa Pullar, Julie Wyatt, Evelyn Apostolou, and Doreen Virtue.

Contents

Acknowledgements v

Introduction ix

Yoga-Based Relaxation (Yoga-Nidra-Style Progressive Relaxation) 1

Healing Meditation – Golden Healing Light Meditation 7

Pranayama/Breath-Flows Awareness (Nadi Shodhan Awareness Exercise) 11

Prana Mudra Visualisation 13

Moon/Sun Breath – Breathing Silver (Moon) Energy up the Body and Golden (Sun) Energy down the Body 17

Visualisation – Breathing into a Flower at Your Navel 21

Visualisation – The Space Within the Heart 23

Yoga Chakra Meditation 1 27

Yoga Chakra Meditation 2 (Shorter Version) 37

Visualisation – Your Special Place or Sanctuary 45

Generic (Short) Introductory Relaxation – For Meditations and Visualisations 49

Visualisation – Flower Garden and Fountain 51

Visualisation – Country Lane, Meadow and Rolling Hills Vista 55

Visualisation – Walk by a River Leading to a Rocky Gorge with a Waterfall 59

Visualisation – Temple of Healing in a Woodland Clearing 65

Visualisation – Moonlit Beach, White Horse and Magical Journey 69

Guided Meditation/Visualisation – Meeting and Connecting
with Your Spirit Guides and Angels 73

Goal Visualisation and Realisation (Including New/Future
Self-Image) 79

Short Relaxation and Visualisation for Beginning a 1-to-1
Energy / Spiritual / Reiki Healing Session 87

Group Meditation for Distant and World Healing 93

About the Author 99

Other Books by Amanda Jackson-Russell 101

Introduction

This book presents a comprehensive series of meditation scripts for general personal use and also for use by tutors, teachers, workshop leaders and student practitioners of spiritual and energy healing, Reiki, yoga and meditation, stress management, relaxation skills, and holistic therapies. It may also be of interest to wellbeing coaches, psychotherapists, hypnotherapists and others involved in mind-body-spirit healing and wellbeing. For personal use, you may find it helpful to record a particular script you are drawn to, so that you can listen peacefully to an audio of it without having to refer constantly to or remember the written script.

IMPORTANT NOTE: Whether reading and practising on your own, recording a script for self-use, or reading a script to clients/students, I would just like to emphasise the following: Read the script SLOWLY and CLEARLY! Make sure you give yourself or your client/students enough time to hear, internalise and respond to the instructions. There is nothing worse than a teacher, practitioner or recording that seems to proceed at lightning speed, so that the listener ends up just giving up trying to follow things! If you are reading/using the script for others, a good measure is to observe the client's/student's breathing rate, matching it accordingly with the readings and instructions, and incorporating appropriate pauses.

The book begins with relaxation and meditation practices drawn from Hatha yoga and spiritual healing, and moves on gently to introduce the reader to working in meditation with the energy centres (chakras) of the body.

The middle part of the book is taken up with a series of visualisations – journeys in the mind and imagination that help to accentuate the senses and allow the participant to enjoy "mini-mind vacations" – to transport themselves to another place and time where they can feel peaceful, relaxed, released from everyday worries and concerns, and restore their mental, emotional and physical balance and vitality.

Towards the end of the book are some more in-depth healing practices, which include: a meditation script to help the participant connect with their spiritual guides and angels, to receive comfort, support and guidance; an empowering process to address one's goals and desired personal and life changes; a short relaxation and visualisation that can be used as a prelude to a one-to-one energy/spiritual/Reiki healing session; and finally a group meditation enabling participants to connect with spiritual healing energies in a safe, protected, grounded way, and send these healing energies out to loved ones, the rest of the world, and beyond.

These writings and scripts have been personally developed over a period of more than 30 years, and I am truly blessed and grateful for the teachings that inspired them. (Ideas for some of the meditations were developed years ago and have only recently made it onto paper; others have developed and evolved over time.) My everlasting gratitude goes in particular to the amazing teachers, course and workshop leaders and other members of the National Federation of Spiritual Healers (NFSH; now The Healing Trust), the British Wheel of Yoga (BWY), Hay House, the College of Psychic Studies, the Spiritualist Association of Great Britain, the Satyananda School of Yoga, the Quantum Edge Healing Institute, and various hypnotherapy resources and organisations. There have been many other sources of insight and inspiration too numerous to mention, and I am so appreciative of them all – it has been and continues to be a wonderful journey. I hope whoever reads this book and puts the exercises to use will greatly enjoy them and gain as much benefit from them as I have.

Amanda Jackson-Russell, 2021.

Yoga-Based Relaxation
(Yoga-Nidra-Style Progressive Relaxation)
– For Relaxation, Peacefulness and Stillness –

[Preparation]
This practice can be carried out either sitting in a chair or lying down in savasana (the corpse pose in yoga). Make sure you will be undisturbed for the duration of the practice. (Remember to turn off any mobile phone and other communications devices, and put any other phone on silent mode.) Also, loosen any belt or tight waist-band, so that you will be able to breathe deeply and easily right down into the lowest parts of your lungs, by allowing your tummy to expand on the in-breath.

[IF SITTING:]
If sitting, make sure you are comfortable and that your spine is straight and your back is well supported. Make sure you will be warm enough. Have your legs uncrossed and a little way apart. Rest your feet flat on the floor or on a pillow. Then just allow your legs to relax as much as possible. Rest your hands comfortably in your lap or on your thighs with the palms facing upwards. (Alternatively, have your hands in a meditation mudra, if that is what you are used to doing or prefer.) Then just allow your arms and shoulders to relax as much as possible. Gently close your eyes. Make sure your jaw is loose and relaxed. Make any final adjustments to your posture now. Then allow your body to be still and rest. For a few moments, focus your attention on the flow of your breath and allow your breathing to settle down into a slow, gentle, even rhythm. And just allow your whole body to rest and relax.

[IF LYING DOWN:]
If lying down, make sure you will be warm enough. (Cover yourself with a blanket if you wish.) Make sure your spine is straight. Have your legs straight if possible. (If that's not comfortable, place a pillow under your knees.) Have your feet about hip-width apart, then relax your legs and allow your toes to flop outwards so that the hips are open. Have your arms resting by your sides a little way from the body, with the palms of the hands facing upwards. (This allows the shoulders to relax and the shoulder blades to rest flat against the floor or couch; it also allows your chest to be open and your breathing unrestricted.) Then just allow your arms and shoulders to relax as much as possible. Rest your head on a folded blanket or thin-ish pillow. Lengthen the back of your neck, so that your chin is tucked in slightly (but don't force the chin down), then let your chin "spring" back to a relaxed position. Gently close your eyes. Make sure your jaw is loose and relaxed. Make any final adjustments to your posture now. Then allow your body to

be still and rest. For a few moments, focus your attention on the flow of your breath and allow your breathing to settle down into a slow, gentle, even rhythm. Just allow your whole body to rest and relax.

[Relaxation – Part 1 – Body/Breath Awareness]
You are now going to relax more deeply by systematically rotating your awareness around your body. This process helps to distract and quieten the analytical parts of the brain, and allows the parts of the nervous system concerned with rest and relaxation to kick in. As each part of the body is mentioned in turn, just bring your attention to that part, without trying to do anything else.

So… Just become aware of your right hand, then your wrist, lower arm, elbow, upper arm, and right shoulder… Then be aware of your armpit, the right side of your chest, the side of your waist, then your right hip… Then take your awareness down your right leg, becoming aware of your thigh – the front of the thigh, the back of the thigh – then your knee, the back of the knee, the shin, the calf muscles… Then your right ankle, the top of your foot, your heel, the sole of the foot, then all of your toes…

Now become aware of your left hand, then your wrist, lower arm, elbow, upper arm, and left shoulder… Then be aware of your armpit, the left side of your chest, the side of your waist, then your left hip… Then take your awareness down your left leg, becoming aware of your thigh – the front of the thigh, the back of the thigh – then your knee, the back of the knee, the shin, the calf muscles… Then your left ankle, the top of your foot, your heel, the sole of the foot, then all of your toes…

Now become aware of your buttocks, and the points of contact with the chair, couch or floor. Now bring your awareness to the base of your spine, then your lower back… the middle of the back… the upper back… Then be aware of the whole of your spine, from the base all the way up to the top… then the whole of your back… Take your awareness to the tops of your shoulders, then the back of the neck… Then up over the back of the head… the top of the head… and over the scalp to the forehead…

Be aware of your temples… your eyebrows… your eyes… your ears… the bridge of your nose… your cheeks… the tip of your nose… Now be aware of your lips… your tongue… your jaw… your chin… Allow all the muscles of your face, your eyes, your mouth and your jaw to rest and relax completely…

Now become aware of your throat… the front of your neck… your collar bones… And continue on, taking your awareness down the front of your body… the centre of your chest... the rib-cage... the solar plexus area in the centre of your trunk... your tummy... your lower abdomen... and the groin area...

Now bring your awareness to your breathing... Just become aware of the flow of the breath and the movements of breathing... And allow your tummy to expand gently with each in-breath, and relax back again on the out-breath... And just become aware of and allow this process of gentle breathing from the abdomen, allowing your breathing to settle into a slow, gentle, even rhythm...

And now, start to gradually make your out-breath a little longer and slower... The body naturally relaxes with the out-breath, so lengthening the out-breath helps the body to release tensions and relax more and more...

Lengthening the out-breath also helps to improve the quality of the in-breath, removing stale air from the lungs more efficiently and enabling more life-giving oxygen to be taken in on the in-breath...

And now, with each out-breath, feel as though you are breathing away any and all tensions from the body... With each out-breath, feel as though you are releasing and relaxing your muscles more and more... With each out-breath, feel as though all your nerves and all your internal organs are releasing and relaxing more and more... With each out-breath, feel as though your whole body is releasing and relaxing more and more...

With each out-breath, breathe away any negative feelings, emotions, thoughts and worries... Feel them flowing out of your fingertips and your toes... flowing away and dissolving into nothingness...

With each out-breath, feel as though a huge wave of relaxation is sweeping down your body from the top of your head to the tips of your toes, washing away tensions from your body and washing away any negative emotions, and any thoughts, cares or worries from your mind...

With each out-breath, feel this wave of relaxation sweeping down your whole body, releasing cares, worries, fears, tensions, and any feelings of frustration, sadness, anger, guilt, resentment... anything that is no longer needed... let them just flow away on the out-breath, feel them flowing out of your fingertips and your toes, flowing away and dissolving into nothingness...

[Relaxation – Part 2 – Observing the Thought Processes]
Now take your awareness into your mind... and become an observer of your own thought processes... If you like, imagine a small screen inside your forehead, and imagine watching your thoughts passing across the screen... Notice what thoughts pop into your mind... without getting involved in any of them... Just be a detached observer of your thoughts, an impartial witness... Allowing any thoughts to just come and go... Just observe the activity of your mind in a relaxed, detached way... Acknowledge any thought that comes up, and then just let it go... [Pause...]

And see if you can detect spaces between the thoughts... [Pause...] What is that in the spaces between your thoughts...? Your consciousness...? [Pause...] Your self, simply being... Just resting in peacefulness... [Pause...]

[Relaxation – Part 3 – Peaceful Lake Visualisation]
And now, in your mind, take yourself away to another place... Imagine being beside a still and peaceful lake... Notice the surface of the lake, gently rippling as a soft, gentle breeze whispers over it... Feel the breeze, warm, soft, gentle, against your skin... Now, as the breeze drops, watch the ripples on the surface of the lake become fainter and fainter, as the lake surface smoothes to stillness... Watch the surface become totally still, like glass... [Pause...]

Now see, on the surface of the lake, a pair of pure-white swans, regal and elegant, gliding smoothly, silently and serenely across the lake... See the gentle V-shaped ripples forming in their wakes... And watch as the ripples become fainter and fainter again, as the lake surface smoothes to stillness... Watch the surface become totally still again, like glass... [Pause...]

And as you view the still and peaceful lake... Breathe in peace, and breathe out serenity... Breathe in peace, breathe out tranquillity... Breathe in peace, breathe out joy... Breathe in peace, breathe out love... Breathe in peace, breath out harmony – with yourself and with all beings... Breath in peace, breathe out contentment... [Pause...]

Now, allow the image of the lake to fade... Allow your mind, your consciousness, to drift for a few moments, feeling peaceful and contented... [Pause...]

[Returning Awareness to the Present]
And now, gradually begin to return your awareness to your breathing... Becoming aware of the flow of the breath... the movements of breathing... the sensations of the air entering and leaving your nostrils... [Pause...]

Start to bring your awareness gradually back to your body… and bring with you all those feelings of relaxation, peacefulness and contentedness…

Start to become aware of the sensations of your body – awareness of your body sitting or lying down… the weight and sensations of your body against the chair, couch or floor… Begin to bring your awareness back to the present… awareness of your surroundings… any sounds you can hear… [Pause…]

Start to take a deeper breath now, filling your lungs and expanding your abdomen and chest… then letting the breath go fully and completely… Then another deep breath… And letting it go… And another… Feeling re-energised and renewed…

Bring your awareness back fully now to the present, to your body and your surroundings… Bringing with you all those feelings of relaxation, peacefulness and contentedness… And feeling re-energised and renewed…

Become aware of your fingers and toes, and start to give them a wriggle and a stretch… And now have a good stretch, becoming fully aware of your body again, and opening your eyes… Feeling relaxed, peaceful, contented and renewed…

(Developed from concepts arising during BWY teacher training, 1986–1989.)

Copyright © Amanda Jackson-Russell 2010, 2021

Healing Meditation
– Golden Healing Light Meditation –

[Short Relaxation Induction]
Make sure you are sitting comfortably with your spine straight and your back well supported. Rest your feet flat on the floor (or on a pillow). Rest your hands comfortably in your lap or on your thighs. Close your eyes. And now, just allow your whole body to relax and let go as much as possible… [Pause…]

Now… just become aware of your breathing… the flow of your breath and the gentle movements of breathing… [Pause…]

Allow your tummy to relax and expand gently with each in-breath… and then relax back again on the out-breath… For a few moments, just rest your attention on this process of gentle breathing from the abdomen, allowing your tummy to expand gently on the in-breath… and then relax back again on the out-breath… [Pause...]

And now, for a moment, become aware of the whole of your body, from the top of your head, all the way down through your trunk, to the tips of your toes… [Pause...]

And now, on the next out-breath, imagine a pleasant wave of relaxation sweeping down your body from the top of your head to the tips of your toes, washing away all tensions, cares or worries from your body and your mind… [Pause...]

And now (on the out-breath), imagine another wave of relaxation sweeping down your body… [Pause...]

And again (on the out-breath)… another wave of relaxation sweeping down through your mind and your body, washing away all tensions, cares and worries… Just breathe them away… Feel them flowing out of your fingertips and out of your toes… flowing away and dissolving into nothingness… [Pause...]

And then, bring your awareness back to your breathing… [Pause...]

And.. just allow your breathing now to settle down into its own (slow,) gentle, even rhythm… [Pause...]

[Healing Meditation]

Now, just imagine that your whole body is surrounded and protected by a beautiful sphere of white and golden healing light. Visualise this sphere of light around you, glowing warm and bright. Feel it protecting you, nurturing you, comforting you... enabling you to feel totally safe, secure, warm, peaceful and comfortable. Allow yourself to rest and relax completely in this protective glowing sphere of light, absorbing its warmth, comfort and peace... [Pause...]

Now, imagine a shaft of warm golden healing light shining down on you from above your head... [Pause...]

And now, start to imagine this warm golden healing light beginning to gently flow down through the crown of your head, pouring into your mind and nervous system, warming, healing, calming and re-energising... [Pause...]

Imagine this glowing healing energy as it begins to flow down your spine... And feel it flowing into your neck and around your shoulders... and pouring down through your arms... around and into your wrists... and into your hands and fingers... Feel it warming, healing, calming and re-energising every part it touches, every muscle, every joint, every nerve, every cell... [Pause...]

Imagine this glowing healing light now flowing down through the centre of your body, touching all the organs, every muscle, nerve, tissue and cell... and flowing into and around every cell, healing as it goes, right down to the very molecules and atoms of your being...

Feel it flowing down through your chest, around your heart, around your rib-cage, and the back of your body too... warming, healing, calming, re-energising... Then feel it flowing on down through your solar plexus and around your waist... and on down, flowing around your abdomen and tummy and all the organs there, and around and through every muscle and nerve, every tissue, every cell... warming, healing, calming and re-energising... renewing and revitalising... [Pause...]

Feel this golden healing energy flowing around your pelvis and your hips, your lower back and your buttocks... flowing in and around all the organs, muscles, joints and nerves... all the tissues and cells... warming, healing, calming, re-energising... [Pause...]

Imagine the whole of your body now beginning to glow with vital healing energy... right down to the very cells, and inside the cells, right down to every tiny molecule and atom of your being... [Pause...]

Now feel this golden healing energy beginning to flow down your legs, gently flowing around and down through your thighs, circling and flowing into and around your knees... then on down through your lower legs... warming, healing, calming, re-energising... touching and flowing through every muscle, every joint, every nerve, every tissue, every cell... And feel it flowing on down into and around your ankles and down into your feet... right down into your toes... Feel your legs and feet and toes glowing with golden healing energy... [Pause...]

Now feel the whole of your body... and your whole mind and nervous system and consciousness... glowing with vital golden healing light... Just allow yourself to rest and bathe in this nurturing, loving, comforting, peaceful, healing energy... allowing it to renew, replenish and revitalise every atom of your being... [Long pause...]

And, if there are any particular areas of your body or your mind – or any parts of your being – that you feel need some extra attention... some extra healing... Just direct the healing energy gently to those parts... Feel those areas absorbing the warm, golden, vital healing energy... Feel them relaxing and releasing, feeling nurtured and comforted... Feel all the cells beginning to glow, re-energise, revitalise and renew themselves... Feel this loving, nurturing, healing energy flowing into and around every cell, right down into the very molecules and atoms... until you can see, feel or imagine those areas glowing with healing energy... and you can imagine those areas feeling warm, peaceful, contented, nurtured, healed, re-energised and revitalised... [Long pause...]

And now, imagine what it would feel like for your body and mind, the whole of your being, to feel completely healed and renewed... What would that feel like...? Picture yourself totally whole, totally healed... feeling vital, alive, joyous, free... totally complete... totally contented... Imagine those feelings... Feel those feelings of wholeness, freedom, joy and total wellbeing... [Long pause...]

Now, begin to imagine the golden healing light beginning to flow towards the centre of your body, the centre of your being... Feel it beginning to concentrate in the centre of your body and being... See it beginning to form a shining ball of healing light right in your centre... Allow it to gather here in your centre... until if finally forms itself into just a tiny bright shining point of healing light... Feel this tiny but powerful point of healing light in the very centre of your being... And know that this source of golden healing light is always there… will always be there… right in the centre of your being… Know that you can tap into this loving, healing energy at any time… whenever you want or need to…

Now, just allow yourself drift for a few moments, feeling peaceful, contented, renewed and revitalised… [Long pause…]

[Returning Awareness to the Present]
And now, gradually begin to return your awareness to your breathing… Becoming aware of the flow of your breath… the movements of breathing… the sensations of the air entering and leaving your nostrils… [Pause...]

Start to bring your awareness gradually back to your body… and bringing with you all those feelings of relaxation, healing, peacefulness and renewal…

Start to become aware of the sensations of your body – awareness of your body sitting or lying down… the weight and sensations of your body against the chair, couch or floor… Begin to bring your awareness back to the present… awareness of your surroundings… any sounds you can hear… [Pause...]

Start to take a deeper breath now, filling your lungs and expanding your abdomen and chest… then letting the breath go fully and completely… Then another deep breath… And letting it go… And another… Feeling re-energised and renewed…

Bring your awareness back fully now to the present, to your body and your surroundings… Bringing with you all those feelings of relaxation, healing and peacefulness… Feeling re-energised and renewed…

Become aware of your fingers and toes, and start to give them a wriggle and a stretch… And now have a good stretch, becoming fully aware of your body again, and opening your eyes… Feeling relaxed, peaceful and renewed…

(Developed from concepts arising during NFSH training and attendance at healing development groups, 1986–1990.)

Copyright © Amanda Jackson-Russell 2012, 2021

Pranayama/Breath-Flows Awareness
(Nadi Shodhan Awareness Exercise)

(Adapted and Developed from the Hatha Yoga Practice of Nadi Shodhan [Alternate-Nostril Breathing])

[Introduction]
In the modern world, particularly in Western society, we spend much of our lives involved with "left-brain" activities – analysis, logic, reasoning, intellectualising, planning, worrying, completing our "to do" lists… And over-emphasis on these activities can create an imbalance in the brain's habitual operating mode, leading to a state of chronic stress. Over the long term, this can cause damage to our health and wellbeing, and our general ability to function in the world, relax and simply enjoy life.

In yoga philosophy, the flows of breath (energy or prana) in the right and left nostrils are associated with the left and right sides of the brain (ie. the opposite sides of the brain). Whether or not you are sympathetic with or interested in this philosophy, it is helpful to be aware of what are traditionally considered "left-brain" and "right-brain" activities, with a view to restoring a balance of nervous energies in our being, and greater wellbeing in our body and mind. The following practice helps us to do this.

[Practice]
Sit in a meditative asana (posture) on a folded blanket on the floor (eg. a simple cross-legged position such as sukhasana, the easy pose; or if you are more flexible, padmasana, the lotus pose); or on an upright chair with your back supported and feet flat on the floor. Rest your hands on your thighs (palms up) or in your lap (palms up, left hand in right, left thumb over right). Keep your spine straight, close your eyes, and allow your body to relax as much as possible at this time. Now focus your attention on the rhythm of the natural breath, gentle and slow, from the abdomen. Allow your tummy to expand on the in-breath, and relax back again on the out-breath.

Become aware of the flow of breath in your *right* nostril. This flow of breath (also considered to be energy or prana) is associated with the left side of the brain: logical and analytical thought, sequential activities, deductive reasoning, language and speech, a masculine type of energy, the right side of the body, and physical activity; also the part of the autonomic nervous system called the sympathetic nervous system – associated with activation of the heart and lungs and the "fight-flight" response.

As you observe the flow of breath into and out of the right nostril, become aware of its physical, mental and energetic associations. Imagine and experience the qualities of this energy as you observe the flow of breath in the right nostril.

Now become aware of the flow of breath in your *left* nostril. This flow of breath (energy or prana) is associated with the right side of the brain: creativity, music, art and painting, spatial awareness, dancing, appreciation of Nature, intuition, inspiration, wholism, a feminine type of energy, the left side of the body, and relaxation; also the part of the autonomic nervous system called the parasympathetic nervous system – associated with rest, recuperation and regeneration of the body.

As you observe the flow of breath into and out of the left nostril, become aware of its physical, mental and energetic associations. Imagine and experience the qualities of this energy as you observe the flow of breath in the left nostril.

Now become aware of the flows of breath in *both* nostrils:
- See that together they create a balance of energies, a balance of mental activities, a balance of body and mind…
- Neither too still and lethargic…
- Nor too active, tense and fluctuating…
- But relaxed, dynamic, flowing, efficient, serene and aware…
- A pleasing and nurturing state of balance and harmony.

Be aware of the state of energies within you – and feel/imagine them in balance and harmony. Visualising and experiencing this state of harmony will help you develop it more and more, so that it eventually becomes your natural "default" state of being.

Now return your awareness to the natural breath – observe the natural breath. Gently begin to bring your awareness back to the physical body.

Rub your hands gently against your thighs, bringing your awareness back to the physical sensations of the body. Open your eyes.

[OPTIONAL: As quietly and calmly as possible, lie down in savasana (the corpse pose), covering yourself with a blanket if you wish.]

Copyright © Amanda Jackson-Russell 2021

Prana Mudra* Visualisation
(Invocation of Vitality/Creative [Earth] Energy
and Wisdom [Spiritual] Energy)

Sit comfortably with your spine straight and well supported. Relax your shoulders and arms, and rest your hands on your thighs or in your lap. Have your legs uncrossed, with your feet resting flat on the floor or on a pillow. Have your eyes gently closed.

Become aware of the natural breath… its gentle rhythm and flow… Allow your breath to become slow and even, breathing gently from the abdomen… Allow your tummy to expand gently on the in-breath, and contract back again on the out-breath…

Allow your body to relax as much as possible at this time... Just let go and imagine any and all tensions flowing out of your whole mind and body… Feel as though any thoughts, cares, worries or tensions are flowing out of you from the top of your head to your feet… flowing out of the tips of your toes… and releasing deep down into the Earth… Let the Earth absorb any negativity… to be transformed into a new and positive energy…

With each out-breath, breathe away worries, cares, anxieties, fears, frustration, guilt, anger, sadness… And with each out-breath, imagine and feel any unwanted thoughts and emotions flushing out of you, flowing out and down, to be absorbed and transformed by the Earth…

With each out-breath, feel yourself letting go, and relaxing, more and more...

Now start to visualise your feet rooting you securely to the Earth… Imagine you have roots extending downwards from the soles of your feet right down into the Earth… Feel the quality of the Earth's energy… strong, powerful, supportive, creative, nourishing…

Begin to imagine this powerful, creative energy flowing up your roots into your feet and rising up your body. With each in-breath, imaging you are drawing up this Earth energy ever more strongly. With each out-breath, see it flowing up through your body. With each in-breath, draw it up from the base of your spine… feel it coursing up your spine, through the centre of your body, up your neck, right up to the top of your head… And as you breathe out, feel it spreading out to all parts of your body and mind…

As you visualise this energy flowing upwards through you, take in the qualities of: **Strength, health, stability, vitality, security, nourishment, personal power (magnetism), creativity, worldly knowledge, peace and harmony with the Earth and all creatures, friendship, nurturing, caring...**

Feel these qualities, this powerful energy, spreading out to all parts of your body, nourishing and revitalising every cell, restoring health and vitality to your body, your mind, your nerves, your emotions. Feel it spreading out beyond you (up and out of you like a fountain) and touching everything and everyone around you... [Pause...]

Now begin to visualise a shaft of shining white-gold light above your head, connecting you to the energy of the Cosmos (and the Source), continuing ever upwards, connecting you with the highest levels of consciousness, awareness, higher knowledge, wisdom and unconditional love. Imagine the quality of this (spiritual) energy – lightness, peace, joy, love, healing, contentment, wisdom, oneness with the Universe, bliss...

Begin to imagine this gentle, yet powerful, energy – like a stream of pure white light – flowing down from the top of your head, down your spine. With each in-breath, feel the flow of this healing energy and wisdom ever more strongly. With each out-breath... feel it pouring down from the top of your head, flowing down your spine and spreading out to all parts of your body...

As you visualise this pure white-gold light flowing down through you, take in the qualities of: **Wisdom, mental clarity, calmness, lightness, awareness, detachment, peace, love, contentment, healing, illumination, higher consciousness, enlightenment, stillness, oneness with the Universe, bliss...**

Feel these qualities, this stream of pure white-gold light, flowing to all parts of your body, healing, calming, soothing, peaceful, loving and knowing...

Feel it flowing out beyond you... from your heart, from your fingertips, from every part of you... flowing out into the world... touching everything and everyone around you and beyond... [Pause...]

Now, just breathe naturally and easily as you feel and see these two powerful energies – the Earth energy and the energy of the Cosmos – working together in harmony, and bringing balance and harmony within you... within all parts of your body... in your nervous system and your thoughts... in your emotions and in your very essence... and bringing balance and harmony all around you and out into the world... [Pause...]

Rest in this harmony of energies… feeling it balancing and restoring your entire being… and creating a field of harmonious energy all around you… that emanates out from you and touches everything around you… and extends and radiates out and out… into the world… the Universe… Yet at the same time, forms a field of protection and safety all around you… that is able to transmute any unwanted influences into loving and positive energy… Imagine folding this field of protective energy... love and warmth… closely around yourself like a luxurious swirling cloak…

[Long pause…]

And now… gradually start to bring your awareness back to your body, sitting in the chair… Become aware of the weight of your body, resting deeply in the chair… Start to become aware of the room (or place) you are in… your surroundings… become aware of any sounds… in the room, or outside the room… bringing your awareness back to the present… the here and now… Feel your feet firmly on the floor (or ground)… Feel yourself deeply connected to the ground… and to the Earth below… safe, stable, secure…

Start to take a couple of deeper breaths now… and let them go… starting to re-energise your body and mind… readying your body to move once again… Bring your awareness fully back to the present… and your surroundings… Start to give your fingers and toes a wriggle and a stretch, bringing your awareness fully back to your body… and its physical sensations… If you wish, give your whole body a good stretch… Finally, open your eyes… looking forwards…

And take all that you are out into the world with you…
Om Shanti (Peace).

*Adapted from "Prana Mudra" in "*Asana, Pranayama, Mudra, Bandha*", by Swami Satyananda Saraswati.

Copyright © Amanda Jackson-Russell 2021

Moon/Sun Breath*
– Breathing Silver (Moon) Energy up the Body and Golden (Sun) Energy down the Body –
(and Creating a Healing Sphere of Light)

This practice can be carried out sitting in a straight-backed chair with the spine well supported and the feet flat on the floor; or sitting on a blanket on the ground in a cross-legged position; or lying down on a blanket or yoga mat in savasana (the corpse pose in yoga).

Make yourself comfortable and gently close your eyes. Relax your body as much as possible. Bring your attention to your breath, and focus on gentle, slow, rhythmic breathing from the abdomen. Allow your tummy to expand on the in-breath, and relax back again on the out-breath. [Pause…]

1) On an *in-breath*, imagine you are breathing a *silver* light/energy (moon energy) up the *left* side of your body from the soles of your feet to the crown of your head; and on an *out-breath*, imagine you are breathing a *golden* light/energy (sun energy) down the *right* side of your body from the crown of your head to the soles of your feet. Do this 7 times.

As you do this, imagine the *silver* light has a soothing, peaceful energy, and the *golden* light has a healing, revitalising, nurturing, protective energy. [Pause…]

2) Now, on an *in-breath*, imagine you are breathing a *silver* light/energy (moon energy) up the *right* side of your body from the soles of your feet to the crown of your head; and on an *out-breath*, imagine you are breathing a *golden* light/energy (sun energy) down the *left* side of your body from the crown of your head to the soles of your feet. Do this 7 times.

As you do this, imagine you are creating a peaceful, protective, glowing, healing *circle* of silver and golden light all around you. [Pause…]

3) Now, on an *in-breath*, imagine you are breathing a *silver* light/energy (moon energy) up the *back* of your body from the soles of your feet to the crown of your head; and on an *out-breath*, imagine you are breathing a *golden* light/energy (sun energy) down the *front* of your body from the crown of your head to your feet – and sweeping under your feet. Do this 7 times.

As you do this, imagine you are now extending the circle of light you have created, to form a glowing *sphere* of silver and golden light all around you – that is bathing you in a warm, peaceful, protective, healing energy. [Pause…]

4) Now, on an *in-breath*, imagine you are breathing a *silver* light/energy (moon energy) up the *front* of your body from the soles of your feet to the crown of your head; and on an *out-breath*, imagine you are breathing a *golden* light/energy (sun energy) down the *back* of your body from the crown of your head to your feet – and sweeping under your feet. Do this 7 times.

As you do this, imagine you are completing the formation of the glowing *sphere* of silver and golden light all around you – and that it is completely surrounding and bathing you in a warm, peaceful, protective, healing energy. [Pause…]

Rest in this soothing, comforting, healing energy, allowing your body, your mind, and all your energies to be balanced, recharged and restored… [Long pause...]

[OPTIONAL:]
[Follow this by a short relaxing visualisation, such as the one below (or another of your choice).]
[ALTERNATIVE:]
[Or follow this simply with a silent period of peaceful reflection.]

[Short Visualisation (Hilltop Vista, Lush Green Valley & River Flowing Through It)]
[Now… in your imagination… take yourself to a place in the countryside… amidst rolling grassy green hills… And find yourself walking up a gentle grassy slope… towards the top of a hill… The sun is high overhead, framed by an almost completely blue sky... with just one or two small fluffy white clouds… You feel the sun's welcome warmth on your face… whilst a gentle breeze caresses you… keeping you feeling comfortable and refreshed…

You approach the top of the slope… and all of a sudden, you are met with a wonderful vista before you... the hillside falls away in front of you to reveal a lush green valley, with green hillsides to the left and right... A river winds its way through the valley, like a long snake weaving back and forth… sparkling and reflecting silver and white in the sunshine, and dazzling your eyes… You see, here and there, small farmhouses dotted around the valley… And on the hillsides, you see white blotches… sheep in the fields… and other images… perhaps horses or cows…

As you look out into the distance... towards the horizon... you can almost make out a hazy line of blue-grey, where the river disappears into the distance and meets the sea [/ ocean]...

You find a spot at the top of the hillside to sit down on the soft springy green grass... and toss off your shoes... and you revel in the sensations of the soft grass between your toes...

Here, you can just sit and drink in the gorgeous vista before you...

You breathe in the freshness of the air... the colours... the lush hillsides... the light... the dazzle of the glinting, winding river... the perfect sky... the glorious sun... the peaceful country sights of farms and livestock... and the distant promise of the horizon...

You feel the energies all around you... refreshing you... revitalising you... restoring your body and mind... calming and soothing... vital and alive... You breathe it all in deeply and joyfully... And breathe out fully and deeply, with a wonderful feeling of release... You let the atmosphere and energies restore your mind-body-spirit-soul... with gratitude and affection... feeling connected with all that is around you... [Pause...]

Finally, as you notice the sun has dropped lower in the sky towards the horizon... and the air is becoming a little cooler... you realise it is time to return now from your dreamtime... and return back to everyday awareness...

You now allow the image of the lush green valley and river fade away... along with the rolling green hills... [Pausc...]]

So now... slowly... start to bring your awareness back to your breath... the flow of the natural breath... slow and even... And start to bring your awareness back to your body... sitting in the chair, or sitting or lying on the floor... breathing gently...

Start to take a couple of deeper breaths now... and let them go... starting to re-energise your body and mind... readying your body to move once again in a little while... and starting to bring your awareness back to the present... the room (or place) you are in... remembering your surroundings in the present...

Start to give your fingers and toes a wriggle and a stretch, bringing your awareness back to your body and its physical sensations… And, if you wish, give your whole body a good stretch… Finally, opening your eyes… (and, if you are lying down, come gently up to a sitting position)… Looking forwards once again…

*Inspired by and adapted from teachings by British Wheel of Yoga teacher Di Kendall and Audrey Murr-Copland of The Healing Trust (formerly the National Federation of Spiritual Healers).

Copyright © Amanda Jackson-Russell 2021

Visualisation
– Breathing into a Flower at Your Navel –

Close your eyes, and relax your body as much as possible... Focus on gentle, slow, rhythmic abdominal breathing...

Begin to imagine a flower in bud at your navel. Imagine its size, shape, colour...

Imagine the sun is shining on the flower and the flower is opening up to the warmth and light of the sun. See the shape of the flower, the colour of the petals... imagine its perfume... feel the warmth and light of the sun on the petals...

Breathe this warmth and light into the flower, and into your navel... Imagine warmth, light, nourishment and healing flowing into your navel... allow it to flow around your abdomen and down your legs to your feet... warm, glowing, healing, soothing...

Allow this warm, glowing energy to flow upwards from your navel into your chest, swirling around, warming, soothing, healing everything it touches... feel it flowing around your shoulders and down your arms to your hands and fingers... and feel it flowing up your spine and neck, into your head and around your face... soothing, calming and healing...

Feel your whole being glowing, warm and relaxed... feeling calm, strong and serene... [Pause...]

Take your awareness back to your navel, and once again be aware of healing energy entering your navel as you breathe in... and then, as you breathe out, feel you are breathing energy out of the back of your waist... and feel as though the energy emerging from the back of your waist is swirling around you... starting to form a cocoon around you... flowing up one side of your body and down the other... and flowing up the front of your body and down the back... creating a wonderful healing protective energy field all around you...

Keep breathing in this way... feeling the energy enter your navel... and exit the back of your waist... and forming this glowing cocoon of energy all around you...

Rest in its protection and nourishment, healing and peace... [Pause...]

After a while, bring your attention back to your navel, and the image of the flower at your navel…

Breathe in all the energy and healing you need... take it deep inside... breathe it in deeply... feel it being stored deep inside of you – condensing into a tiny but powerful point of light at your centre... a powerful store-house of healing energy that you can access at any time you need it, now and in the future…

And now, observe the flower again, and see it gradually closing up its petals, returning back to a bud…

Allow the image of the bud to fade now...

But retain the feelings of peace, calm, health, strength and serenity...

Enjoy the feelings... Then, when you are ready, start to return your awareness to the whole of your body... and your breathing...

And take a couple of deeper breaths now... And when you are ready, slowly open your eyes, looking forwards again... And, if you want to, have a good stretch... Feeling good...

Copyright © Amanda Jackson-Russell 2021

Visualisation
– The Space Within the Heart –

[OPTIONAL:]
Place a small table in front of you, about 1 to 2 metres away. Light a candle and place it on the table.

[SITTING IN A CHAIR:]
Sit in an upright chair with your spine straight and well supported. Have your legs uncrossed and your feet flat on the floor or resting on a pillow. Rest your hands in your lap or on your thighs with the palms facing upwards.

[ALTERNATIVE: SITTING CROSSED-LEGGED ON THE FLOOR:]
Sit cross-legged on a folded blanket with your spine straight. It may be more comfortable if you place a shallow cushion under your buttocks. Rest your hands in your lap or on your thighs with the palms facing upwards.

Close your eyes. Allow your body to relax and let go. Breathe gently from the abdomen, and begin to extend the out-breath a little. With each out-breath, breathe away all tensions, thoughts, worries and cares. With each out-breath, feel your body relaxing and releasing more and more, from the top of your head, down to the tips of your toes.

Now focus your attention on the area of your heart, becoming aware of a point in the centre of your chest. (There are subtle energy centres within the body that can act as gateways to different levels of consciousness – one of these energy centres is in the area of the heart. Focus your attention on the heart centre.)

Imagine there is a little space within the heart centre, and imagine that this space is expanding and you are inside this space. Imagine you are in this little room in the heart centre. There is a candle flame in the centre of the room... Focus your attention on the light of the flame... The light expands, becoming brighter and brighter, filling the whole room... brighter and brighter... filling your consciousness... The light has a quality, a feeling, of peace, contentment, harmony and unconditional love...

The space too seems to be expanding, further and further outwards... and the light increases in intensity, expanding more and more, filling the space, and projecting further and further outwards...

Soon you are enveloped by this dazzling, benevolent light... As you focus on this light and allow it to envelope you, you start to feel as though you are merging with it... It is part of you, you are part of it, and part of everything it touches... You experience a feeling of deep peace, contentment and harmony (and unconditional love)...

You are happy to rest in its stillness... feeling safe and secure... content and peaceful...

You allow yourself to enjoy the feelings... the experience... the energies... You allow yourself to exist, for a while, in this source of universal energy... this energy of peace, healing, love and wisdom... To just be... [Pause...]

Gradually, you come to realise that this source of light, this peace, is within you. You can access it, tap into it, whenever you want to, whenever you need to. It is part of you. It is your centre... and your connection to All That Is...

You allow your whole being to connect with and absorb all this beautiful, nurturing, peaceful, healing and harmonious energy... Breathing it in deeply... And releasing on the out-breath... And with a deep sense of love and benevolence, you send this energy out to the whole of creation... to every living organism on this planet... to every living being... out to the whole universe... sending love and light out everywhere...

[Long pause...]

Now, it is time for you to start to return to the present... to the state of everyday living... But you can keep all these feelings of peace, love, wisdom, benevolence and healing deep within you... Draw these feelings deep inside of you... knowing that you can always tap into these energies... not only for your own healing and wellbeing... but that you can also project them outwards, at any time, to anyone and anything that is in need... [Pause...]

So now, allow the image of the space within the heart to fade... gently... into a mist... Begin to bring your awareness back to the present... but also bring with you those feelings of peace, stillness and contentment, all the qualities of the light within the heart...

Become aware once again of the natural breath... the breathing process... the gentle in-breath and out-breath... and gradually bring your awareness back to your body... Become aware once again of your body sitting here in the chair (or on the floor)... and becoming aware once again of the room you are in...

Become aware of the weight of your body (in the chair, or sitting on the floor)… the sensations of the body… Start to become aware of your fingers and toes… and start to give them a wriggle and a stretch… bringing your awareness back fully to your body. Feel yourself firmly in contact with the floor (/ground).

Now rub the palms of your hands briskly together until they are warm, then hold your palms in front of your eyes, so your eyes can feel the warmth… then slowly remove your hands from in front of your eyes and rest them down again in your lap… Slowly open your eyes, looking forwards once again…

Copyright © Amanda Jackson-Russell 2021

The Main Chakras (Energy Centres) of the Body

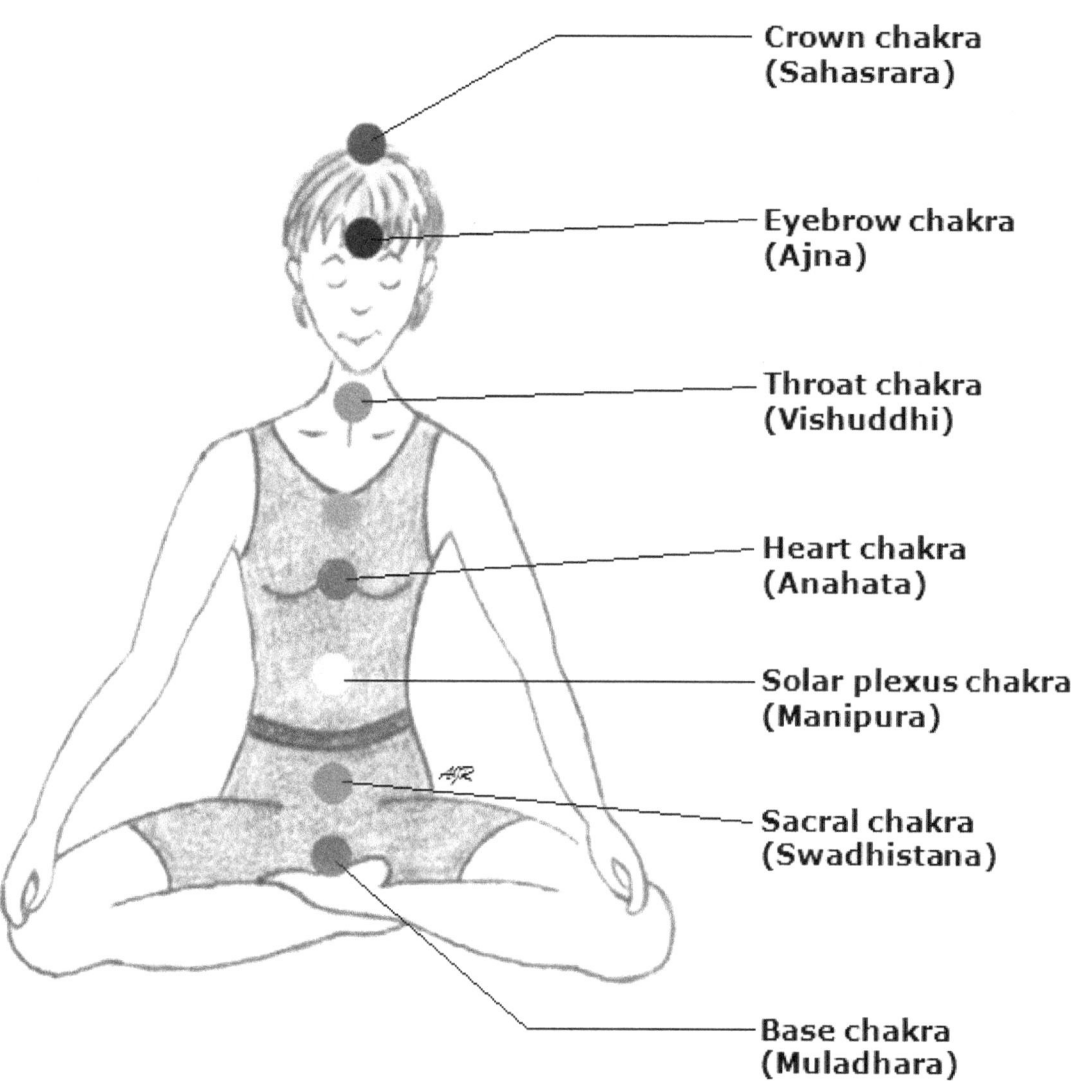

Copyright © Amanda Jackson-Russell 2018, 2021

Yoga Chakra Meditation* 1

[Introduction]

This meditation is a tantric yoga practice involving moving subtle energies. Its purpose is to enable you to:

1) become aware of the main energy centres (chakras) of the body, of which there are seven, aligned along the length of the spine and head, from the base of the spine to the crown of the head;

2) become aware of the purest ("healthy") energetic colours of each chakra;

3) become aware of the physical location of each chakra, and the physical body systems each is associated with;

4) become familiar with the mental, emotional, spiritual and energetic qualities associated with each chakra;

5) experience the various energy levels;

6) experience moving energy to different levels of vibration, from earth energies at the base, to "higher" universal energies at the crown (and beyond);

7) carry out this practice in a controlled, safe and comfortable way, at your own pace;

8) and finally, bring the energy levels back down again from the spiritual/"celestial" to the physical, and ground them, so that you can remain safe in the physical realm, and eventually learn to use these energies safely and constructively in the world and in your life.

[Preparing]

This meditation can be carried out sitting in a chair with good back support, having a straight spine, legs (uncrossed) resting flat on the floor or on a pillow, hands resting comfortably in your lap, and eyes gently closed;

OR

It can be carried out sitting comfortably cross-legged (or in the lotus position, if you are comfortably able to do this) on a folded blanket on the floor (it may be more comfortable if you also place a shallow cushion under the back of your buttocks), with your back straight, hands resting comfortably in your lap or on your knees in a meditation mudra (gesture), and your eyes gently closed.

Allow yourself to settle down and feel relaxed and comfortable, making any adjustments to your posture before you adopt a still position. Then just accept your body position and let it be. Become aware of your breathing – the gentle ebb and flow of the breath. Relax your stomach and allow it to expand (relax) on the in-breath and gently contract back again (without any force) on the out-breath. Just observe the flow of the breath – easy and comfortable – for a few moments… [Pause...]

[Centring]

Now, start to imagine that, with the in-breath, you are breathing up the left side of your body, from your feet (or the base of your spine, if you are sitting cross-legged) to the top of your head... and, with the out-breath, imagine you are breathing down the right side of your body, from the top of your head to your feet (or base)... Complete 7 slow comfortable in- and out-breaths in this way... following the course of the breath around your body... Imagine that you are creating an egg-shaped field of energy all around you... Allow yourself to feel centred, balanced and safe in this energy field... [Pause...]

[Connecting with the Base Energy]

[Muladhara – Base Chakra]

Become aware of the energy centre, or chakra, at the base of your spine (called Muladhara in ancient Sanskrit). Its natural healing colour is a deep crimson red. It is connected, on the physical plane, with reproduction, fertility, elimination of waste products, and the legs and feet. On an energetic level, it is connected to our survival, reproduction, feelings of security, creativity, and physical strength.

Breathing gently and easily... connect your awareness to this energy centre... Be aware of its physical location... Then imagine it like a flower... a deep crimson red... its petals opening up and spreading out... like a flower in the joyous warmth of the sun... Connect to its energetic qualities (survival, reproduction, security, creation, physical strength...) [Pause...]

And now, breathe in deeply... then, as you breathe out, hear the word "Om"... Let it resonate into this energy centre... And once again, take a breath in... and as you breathe out, allow the word "Om" to resonate in this centre... Do this one more time... [3x breaths and "Om"s.]

[Raising the Energy Up]

[Swadhistana – Sacral Chakra]

Now, take your awareness up to the next energy centre – the sacral chakra (called Swadhistana) – in the centre of the sacrum and pelvis. Its natural healing colour is a vibrant deep orange. It is connected, on the physical plane, with digestion and absorption of nutrients, the adrenal glands, the sympathetic nervous system, the "fight-flight" response, the pelvis and the hips. Swadhistana means "one's own place". On an energetic level, it is connected to our digestion (physical, mental and emotional), our inclination to be a part of a like-minded group of souls, our gut instincts, sociability, sexuality and sensuality, play and fun.

Breathing gently and easily... connect your awareness to this energy centre... Be aware of its physical location... Then imagine it like a flower... a vibrant deep orange... its petals opening up and spreading out... like a flower in the joyous warmth of the sun... Connect to its energetic qualities (gut instincts, group instincts, digestion of information, sensuality, fun and play...) [Pause...]

And now, breathe in deeply... then, as you breathe out, hear the word "Om"... Let it resonate into this energy centre... And once again, take a breath in... and as you breathe out, allow the word "Om" to resonate in this centre... Do this one more time... [3x breaths and "Om"s.]

[Manipura – Solar Plexus Chakra]
Now, take your awareness up to the next energy centre – the solar plexus chakra (called Manipura) – right in the centre of your body, in the area of the solar plexus – a complex and powerful nerve network... Its natural healing colour is a vibrant gold-yellow, shining like the sun. It is connected, on the physical plane, with the liver and gallbladder, the spleen, the nervous link between the gut and the brain, the mid-back and the diaphragm... also the left (so-called analytical, logical) side of the brain... On an energetic level, it is connected to our personal power, ego, self-esteem, sense of individuality, conscious mind, and rational and analytical thought processes.

Breathing gently and easily... connect your awareness to this energy centre... Be aware of its physical location... Then imagine it like a flower... a vibrant gold-yellow... its petals opening up and spreading out... like a flower in the joyous warmth of the sun... Connect to its energetic qualities (self-esteem, personal power, individuality, rationality...) [Pause...]

And now, breathe in deeply... then, as you breathe out, hear the word "Om"... Let it resonate into this energy centre... And once again, take a breath in... and as you breathe out, allow the word "Om" to resonate in this centre... Do this one more time... [3x breaths and "Om"s.]

[Anahata – Heart Chakra]
Now, take your awareness up to the next energy centre – the heart chakra (called Anahata) – in the centre of your chest, in the area of the heart and lungs... Its natural healing colour is a rich grass green... the colour of Nature (and of the Healing Archangel

Raphael). It is connected, on the physical plane, to the heart, the cardiac nerve plexus, the blood circulation, the thymus gland, the lungs, chest and ribs, and the lower arms and hands... On an energetic level, it is connected to the so-called "higher" emotions and vibrations of love, caring, compassion, empathy, understanding, kindness, forgiveness, gratitude, appreciation and healing abilities. It encompasses our abilities to care for others, to receive love and caring, and to form healthy nurturing supportive relationships.

Breathing gently and easily... connect your awareness to this energy centre... Be aware of its physical location... Then imagine it like a flower or a fern... a deep rich green... its petals or fronds opening up and spreading out... in the joyous warmth of the sun... Connect to its energetic qualities (love, compassion, nurturing, forgiveness, sharing, gratitude, healing...) [Pause...]

And now, breathe in deeply.. then, as you breathe out, hear the word "Om"... Let it resonate into this energy centre... And once again, take a breath in... and as you breathe out, allow the word "Om" to resonate in this centre... Do this one more time... [3x breaths and "Om"s.]

[Vishuddhi – Throat Chakra]
Now, take your awareness up to the next energy centre – the throat chakra (called Vishuddhi) – in the area of the throat. Its natural healing colour is a bright sky blue... It is connected, on the physical plane, to the thyroid and parathyroid glands (which help regulate our metabolism), our immune system, the throat, voice, mouth, jaws, teeth, ears, upper airways and lungs, eating and swallowing, the neck, shoulders, upper arms, upper back and vital lower brain areas (the brainstem). On an energetic level, it is connected to our self-expression, ability to communicate, listening and teaching, our innate self-healing and protection, ancestral conditioning, our sense of our own authority, and sense of responsibility.

Breathing gently and easily... Connect your awareness to this energy centre... Be aware of its physical location... Then imagine it like a flower... a bright sky blue... its petals opening up and spreading out... like a flower in the joyous warmth of the sun... Connect to its energetic qualities (communication, self-expression, authority, responsibility, self-healing abilities, ancestors...) [Pause...]

And now, breathe in deeply... then, as you breathe out, hear the word "Om"... Let it resonate into this energy centre... And once again, take a breath in... and as you breathe out, allow the word "Om" to resonate in this centre... Do this one more time... [3x breaths and "Om"s.]

[Ajna – Eyebrow Chakra]

Now, take your awareness up to the next energy centre – the eyebrow chakra (called Ajna) – just behind the centre of the forehead, or just above and behind the centre of the eyebrows – also known as the third-eye chakra. Its natural healing colour is a deep, velvety indigo-purple, like the colour of the night sky. It is connected, on the physical plane, to the pituitary gland (which is the body's master gland, regulating hormone levels and many body systems), the middle parts of the brain, the right (so-called creative, intuitive) side of the brain, and the parasympathetic nervous system (which is responsible for rest, relaxation and recuperation). On an energetic level, it is connected to our intuition, imagination, right-brain activities (such as art, music and poetry), memories, subconscious mind, and psychic abilities.

Breathing gently and easily... connect your awareness to this energy centre... Be aware of its physical location... Then imagine it like a flower... a deep indigo-purple... its petals opening up and spreading out... like a flower in the joyous warmth of the sun... Connect to its energetic qualities (imagination, intuition, the creative mind, memories, psychic abilities...) [Pause...]

And now, breathe in deeply... then, as you breathe out, hear the word "Om"... Let it resonate into this energy centre... And once again, take a breath in... and as you breathe out, allow the word "Om" to resonate in this centre... Do this one more time... [3x breaths and "Om"s.]

[Sahasrara – Crown]

Now, take your awareness up to the next energy centre – the crown chakra (called Sahasrara) – just above the crown of the head... Sahasrara is also known as the "thousand-petalled lotus"... Its natural healing colours are ultraviolet, gold and pure white. It is connected, on the physical plane, to the mystical pineal gland, the higher brain areas, and consciousness. On an energetic level, it is connected to higher wisdom, inspiration, spirituality, the "transpersonal", the "superconscious", Universal consciousness. It is not so much a chakra or energy centre – it is more a gateway to higher consciousness and our connection with the Divine, the Source... of the highest wisdom, love, light and healing...

[Connecting with the "Higher" Energy]

[Sahasrara – Crown]

Breathing gently and easily... connect your awareness to the crown centre... Be aware of its physical location... Then imagine it like a flower... but more than a flower... A violet flame of iridescent healing energy, surrounded by brilliant white light... Imagine its many petals opening up and spreading out... like a beautiful luminescent gold-white flower – the "thousand-petalled lotus" – in the joyous warmth of the sun... Connect to its energetic qualities (inspiration, Spirit, love, light, healing, Divine wisdom, Universal consciousness...) [Pause...]

And now, breathe in deeply... then, as you breathe out, hear the word "Om"... Let it resonate into this energy centre... And once again, take a breath in... and as you breathe out, allow the word "Om" to resonate in this centre... Do this one more time... [3x breaths and "Om"s.]

[Experience the Flow of Energies]
And now... focus on your spine, the central column of your body... And as you breathe in, imagine and feel the myriad colours of energy coursing up your spine to the crown of your head... and as you breathe out, imagine and see those energies flowing up out of your crown and all around you, and coursing down the outside of your body...

Feel this wonderful flow of rainbow energies and light flowing up your spine, cascading out of your crown, and flowing out and down over your whole body... your whole being... bathing you in an amazing kaleidoscope of light and colours and healing energies...

Follow this process... As you breathe in, feel the energy coursing up your spine to the crown of your head... And as you breathe out, see those energies flowing up out of your crown and all around you, and coursing down the outside of your body and swirling all around you... Forming a beautiful sphere of energy and radiant light all around you... Protecting, loving, nurturing, healing...

Bask in these radiant energies for a while... absorbing the loving, healing, nurturing energies... [Long pause...]

[Taking the Energies Back Down Again]

[Crown Chakra]
Now, take your awareness back up to the crown chakra, feeling your connection once again with the Universal Divine Source of light, love, wisdom and healing...

You are now going to start the process of bringing the energy down again, to the physical level... starting at the crown, and gradually bringing the energy down through each of the chakras in turn... spending as much time as you need to, to "close down" each chakra... (You will not be closing them completely – but just to a sufficiently safe level...)

Using your breath, imagine you are breathing slowly and deeply into and out of the crown chakra... and as you do so, see the crown chakra as a flower, the petals beginning to close up... closing up tightly... and see it turning (condensing) into a jewel – a brilliant purple-violet amethyst... surrounded by a halo of bright-white diamonds...

Take as much time as you need to bring the energy down... to "close down" the crown chakra... [Pause...]

[Eyebrow Centre]
Then take your awareness down to the eyebrow chakra, just behind the forehead... imagine you are breathing slowly and deeply into and out of this energy centre... and as you do so, see the eyebrow centre as a flower, the petals beginning to close up... closing up tightly... and see it turning (condensing) into a jewel – a deep iridescent blue sapphire – like the velvety midnight sky shining with a billion stars...

Take as much time as you need to bring the energy down... to "close down" the energy of this centre to a safe level... [Pause...]

[Throat Centre]
Then take your awareness down to the throat chakra... imagine you are breathing slowly and deeply into and out of this energy centre... and as you do so, see the throat centre as a flower, the petals beginning to close up... closing up tightly... and see it turning (condensing) into a jewel – a brilliant sky-blue topaz...

Take as much time as you need to bring the energy down... to "close down" the energy of this centre to a safe level... [Pause...]

[Heart Centre]
Then take your awareness down to the heart centre, at the centre of your chest... imagine you are breathing slowly and deeply into and out of this energy centre... and as you do so, see the heart centre as a flower, the petals beginning to close up... closing up tightly... and see it turning (condensing) into a jewel – a regal rich green emerald...

Take as much time as you need to bring the energy down... to "close down" the energy of this centre to a safe level... [Pause...]

[Solar Plexus Centre]
Then take your awareness down to the solar plexus centre, just below the ribs... imagine you are breathing slowly and deeply into and out of this energy centre... and as you do so, see the solar centre as a flower, the petals beginning to close up... closing up tightly... and see it turning (condensing) into a jewel – a gloriously glowing deep yellow citrine...

Take as much time as you need to bring the energy down... to "close down" the energy of this centre to a safe level... [Pause...]

[Sacral Centre]
Then take your awareness down to the sacral chakra, at the centre of the abdomen... imagine you are breathing slowly and deeply into and out of this energy centre... and as you do so, see the sacral chakra as a flower, the petals beginning to close up... closing up tightly... and see it turning (condensing) into a jewel – a rare and vibrant deep orange sapphire...

Take as much time as you need to bring the energy down... to "close down" the energy of this centre to a safe level... [Pause...]

[Base Centre]
Finally, take your awareness down to the base chakra, at the base of the spine... imagine you are breathing slowly and deeply into and out of this energy centre... and as you do so, see the base chakra as a flower, the petals beginning to close up... closing up tightly... and see it turning (condensing) into a jewel – a fiery blood-red ruby...

Take as much time as you need to bring the energy down... to "close down" the energy of this centre to a safe level... [Pause...]

[Centring Once Again]
Now, breathing gently... become aware once again of the energy field all around you... like an egg-shape... closer in to the physical body now... Centre yourself in its protective energy... [Pause...]

[Honouring and Grounding the Energy]
When you are ready, bring your hands together in a prayer gesture... take them up over your head, just above your crown... then, keeping the palms together, slowly lower your hands down... in front of the forehead, then the throat, the heart, the solar area... then allow your hands to turn, pointing the fingers downwards, as your lower your hands past the sacral centre to the base of the spine... pointing your fingers downwards towards the Earth and bowing your head as you fully ground the energy...

[IF SITTING IN A CHAIR:]
Finally, separate your hands and rest them in your lap or on your thighs, with the palms down... Raise your head level again... Then, when you are ready, gently open your eyes, looking forwards...

[ALTERNATIVE/IF YOU ARE SITTING CROSS-LEGGED ON THE FLOOR:]
Bow your head, taking it down towards the floor (if possible/comfortable), and stretch your (praying) hands out in front of you along the ground/floor. (If possible/comfortable, your bottom, knees, head and hands should all be touching the floor.) Then, slowly bring yourself up again to a vertical spine position... Separate your hands and rest them palms-down on your thighs... And when you are ready, gently open your eyes, looking forwards...

*Adapted from teachings by Swami Dayamurti/Doriel Hall (1986–1989), former Diploma Course Tutor with the British Wheel of Yoga.

Copyright © Amanda Jackson-Russell 2021

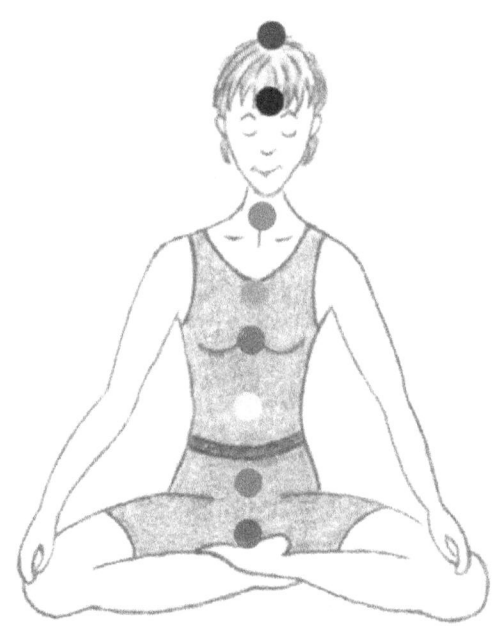

Copyright © Amanda Jackson-Russell 2018, 2021

Yoga Chakra Meditation* 2
(Shorter Version)

This meditation is a slightly shorter version of "Yoga Chakra Meditation 1", described earlier.

[Preparing]
Begin by sitting comfortably in a chair with your back straight and well supported. Rest your feet flat on the floor or on a pillow. Rest your hands comfortably in your lap, and have your eyes gently closed.

[ALTERNATIVE:]
If you prefer, sit comfortably in a cross-legged position on a folded blanket on the floor. Make sure your spine is straight. Have your hands resting comfortably in your lap, or on your knees in a meditation mudra (gesture), and have your eyes gently closed.

Allow yourself to settle down and feel relaxed and comfortable, making any adjustments to your posture before you take up a still position. Then just accept your body position and let it be. Become aware of your breathing – the gentle ebb and flow of the breath. Relax your stomach and allow it to expand (relax) on the in-breath and gently contract back again (without any force) on the out-breath. Just observe the flow of the breath – easy and comfortable – for a few moments… [Pause...]

[Centring]
Now, start to imagine that, with the in-breath, you are breathing up the left side of your body, from your feet (or the base of your spine, if you are sitting cross-legged) to the top of your head... and, with the out-breath, you are breathing down the right side of your body, from the top of you head to your feet (or base)... Complete 7 slow comfortable in- and out-breaths in this way... following the course of the breath around your body... Imagine that you are creating an egg-shaped field of energy all around you... Allow yourself to feel centred, balanced and safe in this energy field… [Pause...]

[Connecting with the Base (Earth) Energy, then Raising the Energy Up]

[Muladhara – Base Chakra]
Become aware of the energy centre, or chakra, at the base of your spine (called Muladhara in ancient Sanskrit).

Breathing gently and easily... connect your awareness to this energy centre... Be aware of its physical location... Then imagine it like a flower... its petals opening up and spreading out... like a flower in the joyous warmth of the sun... [Pause...]

And now, breathe in deeply... then, as you breathe out, hear the word "Om"... Let it resonate into this energy centre... And once again, take a breath in... and as you breathe out, allow the word "Om" to resonate in this centre... Do this one more time... [3x breaths and "Om"s.]

[Swadhistana – Sacral Chakra]
Now, take your awareness up to the next energy centre – the sacral chakra (called Swadhistana) – in the centre of the sacrum and pelvis.

Breathing gently and easily... connect your awareness to this energy centre... Be aware of its physical location... Then imagine it like a flower... its petals opening up and spreading out... like a flower in the joyous warmth of the sun... [Pause...]

And now, breathe in deeply... then, as you breathe out, hear the word "Om"... Let it resonate into this energy centre... And once again, take a breath in... and as you breathe out, allow the word "Om" to resonate in this centre... Do this one more time... [3x breaths and "Om"s.]

[Manipura – Solar Plexus Chakra]
Now, take your awareness up to the next energy centre – the solar plexus chakra (called Manipura) – right in the centre of your body, in the area of the solar plexus.

Breathing gently and easily... connect your awareness to this energy centre... Be aware of its physical location... Then imagine it like a flower... its petals opening up and spreading out... [Pause...]

And now, breathe in deeply... then, as you breathe out, hear the word "Om"... Let it resonate into this energy centre... And once again, take a breath in... and as you breathe out, allow the word "Om" to resonate in this centre... Do this one more time... [3x breaths and "Om"s.]

[Anahata – Heart Chakra]
Now, take your awareness up to the next energy centre – the heart chakra (called Anahata) – in the centre of your chest.

Breathing gently and easily... connect your awareness to this energy centre... Be aware of its physical location... Then imagine it like a flower... its petals opening up and spreading out... [Pause...]

And now, breathe in deeply... then, as you breathe out, hear the word "Om"... Let it resonate into this energy centre... And once again, take a breath in... and as you breathe out, allow the word "Om" to resonate in this centre... Do this one more time... [3x breaths and "Om"s.]

[Vishuddhi – Throat Chakra]
Now, take your awareness up to the next energy centre – the throat chakra (called Vishuddhi) – in the area of the throat.

Breathing gently and easily... connect your awareness to this energy centre... Be aware of its physical location... Then imagine it like a flower... its petals opening up and spreading out... [Pause...]

And now, breathe in deeply... then, as you breathe out, hear the word "Om"... Let it resonate into this energy centre... And once again, take a breath in... and as you breathe out, allow the word "Om" to resonate in this centre... Do this one more time... [3x breaths and "Om"s.]

[Ajna – Eyebrow Chakra]
Now, take your awareness up to the next energy centre – the eyebrow chakra (called Ajna) – just behind the centre of the forehead, or just above and behind the centre of the eyebrows (also known as the third-eye chakra).

Breathing gently and easily... connect your awareness to this energy centre... Be aware of its physical location... Then imagine it like a flower... its petals opening up and spreading out... [Pause...]

And now, breathe in deeply... then, as you breathe out, hear the word "Om"... Let it resonate into this energy centre... And once again, take a breath in... and as you breathe out, allow the word "Om" to resonate in this centre... Do this one more time... [3x breaths and "Om"s.]

[Sahasrara – Crown]
Now, take your awareness up to the next energy centre – the crown chakra (called Sahasrara) – just above the crown of the head... Sahasrara is also known as the "thousand-petalled lotus"...

Breathing gently and easily... connect your awareness to the crown centre... Be aware of its physical location... Then imagine it like a flower... but more than a flower... a "thousand-petalled lotus"... Imagine its many petals opening up and spreading out... in the joyous warmth of the sun… [Pause...]

And now, breathe in deeply... then, as you breathe out, hear the word "Om"... Let it resonate into this energy centre... And once again, take a breath in... and as you breathe out, allow the word "Om" to resonate in this centre... Do this one more time... [3x breaths and "Om"s.] [Pause...]

[Feel Rainbow Energies Flowing Up Your Spine]
Now... focus on your spine, the central column of your body... And as you breathe in, imagine and feel a rainbow of colours and energy flowing up your spine to the crown of your head... [OPTIONAL: and as you breathe out, imagine and see those energies flowing up out of your crown and all around you, and coursing down the outside of your body…] [Pause...]

[Connecting with the "Higher" Energies, and Feeling them Harmonise with Your Own Energies]

Keeping your awareness on your crown chakra, become aware now of a sphere of brilliant white-gold light, just above the crown chakra... feel it connecting with your crown... And now imagine and feel this golden-white energy beginning to flow down through your crown... and flow down your spine… spreading out and down to all parts of your body... [Pause...]

And now see this golden-white light energy flowing down your spine, and meeting and blending with the rainbow energies flowing up your spine... Feel the energies intertwine, blend and harmonise... a wonderful flow of brilliant gold and rainbow energies flowing up and down your spine and spreading out to all parts of your body... to all parts of your being… [Pause...]

Take your awareness once again back to your crown... and feel all these energies spilling out of and over the crown... flowing out all around you... coursing down the outside of your body…

Follow this process... On the one hand, feeling the rainbow energies coursing up your spine to the crown of your head... And then, feeling the golden-white light flowing down your spine... mingling and harmonising with the rainbow energy... and then this harmony of energy spilling out of your crown, coursing down the outside of your body and swirling all around you... Forming a beautiful sphere of energy and radiant light all around you... Protecting, loving, nurturing, healing... [Pause...]

Feel this wonderful flow of golden rainbow energies and light cascading out and down over your whole body... your whole being... bathing you in an amazing kaleidoscope of light and colours and healing energies...

Bask in these radiant energies for a while... absorbing the loving, healing, nurturing energies... [Long pause...]

[Taking the Energies Back Down Again]

[NOTE: In the following, you are guided to see each energy centre closing up and turning (condensing) into a bright jewel. Alternatively, if you find this difficult to visualise, or if you need to make the meditation a bit shorter, you can imagine drawing a small circle, then a cross within the circle, over each energy centre.]

[Crown Chakra]
Now, take your awareness back to the crown chakra... (feeling your connection once again with the Universal Divine Source of light, love, wisdom and healing...)

You are now going to start the process of bringing the energy down again, to the physical level, starting at the crown, and gradually bringing the energy down through each of the chakras in turn, spending as much time as you need to, to "close down" each chakra... (You will not be closing them completely – but just to a sufficiently safe level...)

Using your breath, imagine you are breathing slowly and deeply into and out of the crown chakra... and as you do so, see the crown chakra as a flower again, the petals beginning to close up... closing up tightly... and see it turning (condensing) into a sparkling jewel...

Take as much time as you need to bring the energy down... to "close down" the crown chakra... [Pause...]

[Eyebrow Centre]
Then take your awareness down to the eyebrow chakra... imagine you are breathing slowly and deeply into and out of this energy centre... and as you do so, see the eyebrow centre as a flower, the petals beginning to close up... closing up tightly... and see it turning (condensing) into a brilliant jewel...

Take as much time as you need to bring the energy down... to "close down" the energy of this centre to a safe level... [Pause...]

[Throat Centre]
Then take your awareness down to the throat chakra... imagine you are breathing slowly and deeply into and out of this energy centre... and as you do so, see the throat centre as a flower, the petals beginning to close up... closing up tightly... and see it turning (condensing) into a beautiful bright jewel...

Take as much time as you need to bring the energy down... to "close down" the energy of this centre to a safe level... [Pause...]

[Heart Centre]
Then take your awareness down to the heart centre... imagine you are breathing slowly and deeply into and out of this energy centre... and as you do so, see the heart centre as a flower, the petals beginning to close up... closing up tightly... and see it turning (condensing) into a glowing jewel...

Take as much time as you need to bring the energy down... to "close down" the energy of this centre to a safe level... [Pause...]

[Solar Plexus Centre]
Then take your awareness down to the solar plexus centre... imagine you are breathing slowly and deeply into and out of this energy centre... and as you do so, see the solar centre as a flower, the petals beginning to close up... closing up tightly... and see it turning (condensing) into a sparkling jewel...

Take as much time as you need to bring the energy down... to "close down" the energy of this centre to a safe level... [Pause...]

[Sacral Centre]
Then take your awareness down to the sacral chakra... imagine you are breathing slowly and deeply into and out of this energy centre... and as you do so, see the sacral chakra as a flower, the petals beginning to close up... closing up tightly... and see it turning (condensing) into a brilliant jewel...

Take as much time as you need to bring the energy down... to "close down" the energy of this centre to a safe level... [Pause...]

[Base Centre]
Finally, take your awareness down to the base chakra... imagine you are breathing slowly and deeply into and out of this energy centre... and as you do so, see the base chakra as a flower, the petals beginning to close up... closing up tightly... and see it turning (condensing) into a glowing jewel...

Take as much time as you need to bring the energy down... to "close down" the energy of this centre to a safe level... [Pause...]

[Centring Once Again]
Now, breathing gently... become aware once again of the energy field all around you... like an egg-shape... closer in to the physical body now... Centre yourself in its protective energy... [Pause...]

[Honouring and Grounding the Energy]
When you are ready, bring your hands together in a prayer gesture... take them up over your head, just above your crown... then, keeping the palms together, slowly lower your hands down... in front of the forehead, then the throat, the heart, the solar area... then allow your hands to turn, pointing the fingers downwards, as your lower your hands past the sacral centre to the base of the spine... pointing your fingers downwards towards the Earth and bowing your head as you fully ground the energy...

Finally, separate your hands and rest them on your thighs with the palms down... Raise your head level again, and take in a slow deep breath... and let it go... Then, when you are ready, gently open your eyes, looking forwards...

*Adapted from teachings by Swami Dayamurti/Doriel Hall (1986–1989), former Diploma Course Tutor with the British Wheel of Yoga.

Copyright © Amanda Jackson-Russell 2021

Visualisation
– Your Special Place or Sanctuary –

Sit in a quiet place where you will be undisturbed. Have your spine straight and your back well supported. Have your legs uncrossed with your feet flat on the floor or resting on a pillow. Rest your hands in your lap or on your thighs. Make yourself as comfortable as possible. Close your eyes. Allow your body to relax and let go…

Now, in a few moments, you are going to create for yourself, in your imagination, a special place, a sanctuary, where you feel relaxed, comfortable, peaceful and safe. A special place that is all yours, where you can go to in your mind, whenever you want to or need to, to feel safe, peaceful and relaxed.

It can be somewhere you have been to, maybe on holiday, maybe long ago, or just recently. You may have been there only once, or you may have been there many times. Or it may be somewhere totally imaginary, a beautiful place, your ideal place. A place where you feel safe and at ease, where you feel really good. Perhaps somewhere in Nature – a garden, a meadow, a mountain-top or a green valley, or beside a lake, a river or the sea, or in a forest. Or it may be indoors or underground. It could even be under the ocean, on an island, or even on another planet. Somewhere where you feel comfortable, pleasant, safe and peaceful.

So think of somewhere you would enjoy being – that feels peaceful, pleasant and relaxing – and take your time as you create your special place – it is *your* special sanctuary. Imagine your environment, notice the details, objects, colours, sounds, smells, any particular feelings or impressions you get about it. And if at any time, you decide you want to change the details, or even the location, you are free to do so…

You may be alone in your special place, or there may be someone with you – or a special animal or pet. Or there may be a group of friends or family with whom you feel safe, peaceful and at ease. It's your place. You can make it exactly the way you want it. If you want, you can place a special protective bubble around it, a force-field, or a golden light, to keep you and your special place safe and protected, and so that you can allow in only what or whom you want to be in there.

You can do anything you like to make your special place more comfortable and home-like. You might have some type of house, shelter or a sacred temple there. And you can do whatever you like there, be completely free and at ease – laugh, sing, shout, run, dance, sit, lie down, play music, whatever you want. It's a place where your senses seem to come alive – seeing, touching, tasting, hearing, feeling... Where you feel more alive, more vital, more vibrant, more joyful, a wonderful feeling of total wellbeing. You can be completely yourself here – no judgements, no worries or cares or responsibilities, nothing to disturb or frighten or bother you, no one you have to please, nothing you have to do if you don't want to. You can feel totally at ease.

Now just take a few moments to fully imagine all the details of this place... See everything in your mind... look around... and notice what it is about this place that makes you feel good – think about the different sights and sounds... smells... textures... colours... Notice what is happening... what you are doing... how your body feels... Notice your thoughts... your mental and emotional state... in this place... and how they help you to relax and feel good... Notice the feelings of pleasure that it gives you to be here...

And now, imagine feelings of total happiness and contentment... Smile to yourself inside... Noting how wonderful and totally relaxed and content you feel in this place...

And now, just affirm to yourself: ***"I am totally relaxed, peaceful and content."***

Experience and enjoy your special place, your special sanctuary. You deserve this place and it is all yours. Enjoy the feelings – relaxed, comfortable, serene... safe and secure... warm, peaceful, contented... free and easy... confident and at ease with yourself... soothed, nurtured, supported... feeling comforted, restored and healed by the nurturing environment... [Pause...]

From now on, this is your own special sanctuary. You can come here any time you like, just by closing your eyes and desiring to be here. And you will always find it relaxing and healing, peaceful and comfortable, totally safe. It will also be a special place of power for you, where you can draw on positive energy, new vitality, strength, courage, confidence, inspiration and wisdom.

If you want, you can give your special place a name – the actual name of the place, if it's a real location – or another special name that brings it to mind. And whenever you think of that name, you will recall your special sanctuary in all its details, along with all the good feelings you experience here. [Pause...]

And your special place can become a safe place for you to return to whenever, in your daily life, you find yourself caught up in worries or problems or unwanted thoughts or feelings and you want to stop that train of negative thoughts or break out of those negative feelings.

So now, just spend a little while longer here in your special sanctuary... Enjoy all the sights and sounds... all your senses... all the feelings of comfort and peace, calm and ease, safety and security...

[Long pause...]

If you wish, if you give yourself permission, you can take the wonderful feelings you feel in your special place out with you into your everyday life. You can learn how to do this more and more, as you imagine and go to your special place often, and experience the peace, comfort, ease and safety here. [Pause...]

In a moment, you are going to take leave of your special place, knowing you can return here whenever you like. And you are going to bring back with you many of those wonderful feelings, back into your everyday life and your journey through life.

So, gradually now, allow the images of your special sanctuary to fade from your mind... but keep the feelings with you...

Start to become aware of your breathing... the natural breath... Become aware of your body, sitting in the chair... Become aware of the room where you are sitting... gently bringing yourself back to the present now... And when you are ready, open your eyes and have a good stretch... feeling good...

Copyright © Amanda Jackson-Russell 2020, 2021

Generic (Short) Introductory Relaxation
– For Meditations and Visualisations –

This brief relaxation induction is used at the start of the Golden Healing Light Meditation ("Healing Meditation"). It can be used at the start of each of the next five Visualisations, and also other Meditations and Visualisations, where some preparatory or additional relaxation might be beneficial.

[Short Relaxation Induction]
Make sure you are sitting comfortably with your spine straight and your back well supported. Rest your feet flat on the floor (or on a pillow). Rest your hands comfortably in your lap or on your thighs. Close your eyes. And now, just allow your whole body to relax and let go as much as possible… [Pause…]

Now… just become aware of your breathing… the flow of your breath and the gentle movements of breathing… [Pause…] Allow your tummy to relax and expand gently with each in-breath… and then relax back again on the out-breath… For a few moments, just rest your attention on this process of gentle breathing from the abdomen, allowing your tummy to expand gently on the in-breath… and then relax back again on the out-breath… [Pause…]

And now, for a moment, become aware of the whole of your body, from the top of your head, all the way down through your trunk, to the tips of your toes… [Pause…] And now, on the next out-breath, imagine a pleasant wave of relaxation sweeping down your body from the top of your head to the tips of your toes, washing away all tensions, cares or worries from your body and your mind… [Pause…]

And now (on the out-breath), imagine another wave of relaxation sweeping down your body… [Pause…]

And again (on the out-breath)… another wave of relaxation sweeping down through your mind and your body, washing away all tensions, cares and worries… Just breathe them away… Feel them flowing out of your fingertips and out of your toes… flowing away and dissolving into nothingness… [Pause…]

And then, bring your awareness back to your breathing… [Pause…] And… just allow your breathing now to settle down into its own (slow,) gentle, even rhythm… [Pause…]

Copyright © Amanda Jackson-Russell 2012, 2021

Copyright © Amanda Jackson-Russell 2021

Visualisation
– Flower Garden and Fountain –

Imagine you are walking on a soft springy lawn of lush green grass in a beautiful garden, surrounded on either side by beds of pink, yellow, white and red roses, interspersed with low lavender bushes, lilacs, rhododendrons and a myriad of other flowering plants and shrubs of infinite colours and hues. The grass is dewy and there are crystal drops of dew on the rose petals. You walk by the rose blossoms, noting the waxy petals, the intensity or delicacy of the colours and the perfect shapes of the flowers. You reach out to caress a deep pink rose blossom and feel the velvet-like smoothness of the petals.

As the sun rises in the sky and the dew starts to evaporate from the petals, the scents of the various flowers become more intense. You can detect the delicate rose perfumes, the unmistakable aroma of the lavenders, and the heady scent of the lilacs. There are other perfumes, whose flowers you can't immediately locate – lily-of-the-valley, hyacinth, honeysuckle, and others. The green lawn forms a wide carpet between the flower beds, and you walk down the garden, enjoying the sun on your face, the deep blue of the sky, the softness of the grass, the colours and the perfumes around you.

A pebble path leads you down the garden and towards a wooden archway between some taller shrubs. The archway is draped with soft blue clematis flowers, yellow honeysuckle, delicate white jasmine and pale pink climbing roses. As you walk through the archway, you enter a circular garden, with more flower beds around the edges, filled with bright-coloured delphiniums, gladioli, columbines, snapdragons and many more flowers.

Towards the middle of the garden is a splendid fountain, shooting sprays of silver-crystal water up into the air, the droplets cascading back down into the pool below. The fountain is creating a delicate mist around itself and the pool, and the sunlight shining through the mist and glinting off the falling water droplets creates a shimmering rainbow over the area.

One side of the fountain and pool is bounded by a semi-circular wooden bench, on which you sit, to rest in the warm sun. You can lean over the edge of the bench towards the fountain and feel the cool water droplets wash through your fingers. You touch some of the crystal clear water to your face, cooling your forehead – it feels soothing and refreshing. You sit for a while and watch the sprays of water shooting up into the air and the droplets splashing down into the pool below, marvelling at the lights and colours that are created by the sunlight, and breathing in the clean, cool, fresh air around the fountain.

You listen for a while to the splashing and rippling sounds of the spraying water, whilst watching the droplets of water sparkling in the sunlight. The effect of the water and the light seems to have a cleansing and releasing effect on you – you feel as though all tensions, thoughts and cares are being washed away. It is soothing you, calming and relaxing you. It also has a revitalising effect, seeming to restore your energy, refresh and renew you in body and mind. [Pause...]

On the opposite side of the pool, the garden slopes downwards a little, and water flows from the fountain pool through a rocky channel down into a lower larger pool surrounded by small rocks and rock plants. You walk down the grassy slope towards the lower rock pool. It is covered partly by water-lily pads, the occasional waxy white water lily resting serenely on the surface, like a mystical lotus flower. Between the water-lily pads, you can see yellow and orange fish darting about beneath the surface of the water. There's a sudden movement from below the water, and a fat green frog is suddenly resting on a lily pad – he remains motionless for a minute or two, as though basking in the warm sun – then just as quickly, in a flash of movement, he leaps back into the water and disappears below the surface.

To the far side of the rocky pool, between a gap in the rocks and rock plants, is a graceful weeping willow tree, dangling its delicate drooping branches over the edge of the water, some of the catkins brushing the surface of the pool. Under the willow tree is a mound of soft dry grass. The sun has risen higher in the sky now and is quite warm. You make your way around to the willow tree and sit down on the grassy mound under the tree, to rest a while in its shade and enjoy the sights, sounds and scents of the garden. [**OPTIONAL:** For a time, a small bird high in the willow tree warbles cheerfully to you, before taking flight over the flowers and shrubs, off and away.] You breathe in the peace and freshness, allowing the sights, scents and energies of the tree, the water, the fountain and the flowers to wash away any tensions, and restore and renew you. [Pause...]

As the sun starts to sink lower in the sky, it is time for you to take your leave of the tree, the pools of water, the fountain and the gardens. You arise slowly, taking your last look around the circular garden and breathing in the refreshing scented air, then releasing your breath in a deep sigh of contentment. You make your way again over the soft grass towards the wooden archway, noting the scents of the jasmine and honeysuckle. You pass through the archway along the pebble path into the outer garden, and back across the springy green lawn between the rose flower beds.

And now, you gradually allow the image of the garden to fade, as you begin to bring your awareness back to the present – starting to become aware once again of your breathing, the sensation and rhythm of your breath, and starting to remember where you are, the room you are in. You start to become aware once again of your body (sitting in the chair or lying on the floor).

Start to take a couple of deeper breaths now, bringing your awareness back to your body (sitting or lying here in this room), preparing the body to start moving again soon. And once again, take a couple of deeper breaths, re-energising your body and mind. Start to become aware of your fingers and your toes, and start to stretch your fingers and wriggle your toes a little. Bring your awareness back fully to your body, and when you are ready, give yourself a good stretch. When you are ready, gently open your eyes. (If you are lying down, gently roll yourself onto your right side, before carefully and slowly sitting up.) And just sit for a few more moments to make sure you are fully grounded and back in the present.

Copyright © Amanda Jackson-Russell 2021

Copyright © Amanda Jackson-Russell 2021

Visualisation
– Country Lane, Meadow and Rolling Hills Vista –

Find yourself walking along a country lane in late spring. There are high hedges on either side of the lane, interspersed with tall trees sprouting fresh pale green leaves. Some of their branches reach up high overhead and bend over the lane, so that their tops touch in the middle. Every now and then, you hear rustling and chirping in the hedgerows, as wild birds busy about and flit in and out. You catch the scent of mustiness from beneath the hedges and the occasional scents of wild garlic and wild spring flowers. It is a sunny day, and the sunlight flickers down on you in and out of the trees and hedges. A gentle breeze caresses your face. You walk easily and contentedly, enjoying the fresh spring air and peace.

As you continue along, you notice, to one side of the lane, a wooden stile in a gap in the hedges, indicating a footpath. You decide to explore the footpath, and you climb over the low wooden stile. It leads up a gentle grassy slope, beside another hedgerow. You continue up the path and gradually emerge from the relative darkness of the country lane, trees and hedges, as the path reveals a grassy field... and you find yourself now in the full light of the spring sunshine and an expanse of clear blue sky. The sun warms your face and you take in a deep glorious breath of fresh air... and as you breathe out, you feel your whole body relaxing…

As you continue along the path, the view ahead of you reveals a glorious meadow of low lush green grass, interspersed here and there with taller reed-like grasses and masses of meadow flowers – blue cornflowers, golden buttercups, pale yellow cowslips, red clovers, purple thistles, delicate crimson pimpernels and bright red poppies – all nodding and swaying in the warm breeze. You walk easily, feeling the soft springy grass beneath your feet.

You take in the heady scents of the meadow, as well as enjoying the freshness of the air, feeling the warm sun on your face, and wondering at the blueness of the sudden expanse of sky, dotted here and there with high fluffy white clouds. Birds, mostly invisible [or unseen] to you, are singing and warbling joyfully, and you can also hear the chirping of what seems like dozens, if not hundreds, of crickets spread far across the meadow.

Several grassy paths cross the meadow, worn by previous walkers. You chose a path that heads towards a large flat tree stump at what looks like the far edge of the meadow. As you get closer to the dry stump, which is surrounded by a soft mound of grass and moss, you see that it is sited at the top of a grassy slope that falls away on the other side. And you see that the tree stump provides the perfect viewing point for a breath-taking vista of gently rolling hills and fields that are now visible to you. You stop to sit and rest on the tree stump, which feels warm and safe and quite comfortable, with your feet resting in the soft grass.

Before you, you take in an array of colours and shapes – gently rolling hills covered in patchworks of fields of bright yellow, pale gold, and varying hues of green, purple and brown. Here and there, nestling among the fields, you can pick out occasional farmhouses, lines or clusters of trees, and a field or two with lazily moving cows; another with sheep and some playful lambs frisking about. Through shallow valleys between some of the hills and fields, as you focus your eyes far into the distance, you can detect a line of deeper blue on the edge of the horizon, where the sea [or ocean] is just barely visible.

You sit and enjoy this wondrous masterpiece of Nature in front of you and around you – absorbing the colours, the light, the warmth and energy of the sun, the blueness of the sky, the freshness of the scents and the breeze, the busyness and joyfulness of the birds and crickets in the meadow behind you, and also the feelings of peace, harmony and vitality all around you. As you sit, you breathe in all these sensations and energies, and they seem to refresh and revitalise you with every breath. You feel your whole body and being relaxing more and more, and you feel as though all your cares, worries, tensions, aches and pains, and any stresses are being washed out of you, just draining away. You are able to let go completely of thoughts and cares and just allow yourself to be washed and renewed by the feelings, sights, sounds and sensations of peace and harmony around you and before you... And you allow yourself to be re-energised by the vibrancy of the colours, sights and sensations, the healing power of Nature, and the atmosphere around you...

[Long pause...]

After a time, you notice that the sun is now quite low in the sky – a bright orange ball just starting to sink towards the horizon behind the hills and fields, turning the sky and small clouds delicate pink and pale gold, and turning the grass around you a rich deep green. The crickets are quiet now, and the birds are chirping their last songs as they start to take cover in the hedgerows...

The light is beautiful, but it is time now to start making your way back. You get up from the old tree stump, taking in one last image of the rolling hills and the sinking sun. Then you make your way steadily back across the soft grass of the meadow to the pathway alongside the hedgerow from where you started out... back down to the wooden stile... climbing over the stile and back into the country lane... easily tracing your steps back, as the gentle breeze – a little cooler now – accompanies you... You walk back beneath the tall trees overhanging the lane... and the pale orange-gold light flickers through their branches, gently lighting your way...

And now, you gradually allow the image of the country lane to fade, as you begin to bring your awareness back to the present...

Start to become aware once again of your breathing, the sensation and rhythm of your breath... starting to remember where you are, the room you are in... Start to become aware once again of your body (sitting in the chair)...

Take a couple of slow deeper breaths now, bringing your awareness back to your body (sitting here in this room), preparing your body to start moving again soon... and letting the breath go slowly and fully... And again, take a couple of deeper breaths now, re-energising your body and mind... and let the breath go... Start to become aware of your fingers and your toes, and start to stretch your fingers and wriggle your toes a little. Bring your awareness back fully to your body now... feeling good... rested and re-energised... And when you are ready, gently open your eyes, looking forwards... Give yourself a good stretch... And just sit for a few more moments to make sure you are fully grounded and back in the present.

Copyright © Amanda Jackson-Russell 2021

Visualisation
– Walk by a River Leading to a Rocky Gorge with a Waterfall –

Find yourself walking along a rough pathway beside a small river that is on your right-hand side. The river is winding its way through a wide grassy valley, and you are flanked on both sides by grassy pastureland that gently rises on either side to form low hills.

The sun is shining and the sky is a deep blue, dotted here and there with high fluffy white clouds. A gentle breeze brushes your face, keeping you cool and comfortable in the warm sun. As you walk along, you notice the sunlight flashing and sparkling on the surface of the small river as the water bubbles over rocks and around reeds, and around grasses dipping into the water from the banks. You occasionally detect a sudden small splash, as a fish jumps up in the swirls and ripples of the water. A moorhen scuttles across the river to find cover in some water grasses, followed hastily by a little brood of chicks. Dragonflies swoop and dance over the water.

[OPTIONAL:]
[You stop for a second to inspect the water more closely, and you can then see occasional groups of small fish darting here and there under the water, among rocks, pebbles and duckweed. Over the pastureland around you, butterflies alight on grasses and wild flowers, and field martins, like small swallows, swoop and glide in the air, as if performing aeronautical displays for your benefit. The joyful songs of other birds, mostly unseen, carry across the wide grassy valley.]

[ADDITIONAL/OPTIONAL:]
[Continuing on your walk, you momentarily raise your face up to warm it in the sun and smile to yourself, enjoying the peace and the energy of Nature around you. You take in a deep breath of the fresh clean air and let go a sigh of contentment.]

As you continue walking beside the glinting and twinkling water, the path starts to gently slope uphill. High up in the distance ahead of you, you now see a low mountain range, and you realise you are walking upstream towards the source of the water.

The land to your left side is becoming higher, the further you progress, and the pastureland on that side is becoming narrower. As you continue on, you realise that, some way ahead, you can't see where the river goes, because the path seems to disappear as it bends to the left around a steep, high grassy outcrop.

You continue on along the path, getting closer to the grassy outcrop. The path and landscape are becoming more rocky, less grassy, and rock plants, moss and flowers are now starting to appear along the edges of the river and the path. The path is getting a bit steeper and you are higher up now…

[OPTIONAL:]
[You pause for a moment to look back along the path you have travelled along, and you take in the view of the wide grassy valley and the small river winding its way down into the distance, towards the ocean, somewhere far far on the horizon… [Pause…] You turn back again to continue on your journey…]

You are at last coming to the grassy outcrop around which the path and the river turn sharply to the left. As you round the grassy outcrop, the path levels out again and you are all at once met with an awesome sight and the sound of rushing water. Ahead of you is a wide crystal pool of water, brightly lit by the sunlight, surrounded on either side by mossy rocks covered in coloured flowers and bright green rock plants. And cascading into the crystal pool from higher rocks straight ahead and above you is a beautiful curtain of bright sparkling silver water. The waterfall is not huge, but it is not a trickle either, and it is not coming from the greatest of heights, but it does start several feet above your head. It is just enough to feed the small river and create a wonderful, almost personal, little haven of peace, beauty and energy.

The water of the pool is crystal clear with a greenish hue, and it flashes and ripples with gold and blue as it reflects the sun and the blue sky above. The water dances and jumps with white foam where the cascade of water splashes into the pool, throwing up silver droplets and coloured sprays of light. A faint mist hovers over the pool and around the waterfall, and the sunlight shining through the mist casts an ethereal rainbow over the whole area.

The crystal pool is enclosed by white rocks interspersed with patches of soft white sand. You slip off your shoes and socks and carefully step onto a sandy part and test the shallow water at the edges with your toes. The water is surprisingly warm from the sun, and feels comforting and silky. You find a flat rock, warm in the sunlight, where you can sit, dangling and soothing your feet in the clear water. You can dip your hands into the water and wash and soothe your face with the refreshing liquid.

You take in the peace, beauty and serenity of this special place, watching the changing lights and colours as the water splashes and sparkles in the sunlight. You feel the soothing, refreshing silkiness of the water. And you listen to the rushing sound of the waterfall and the bubbling and splashing on the surface of the pool. It seems as though all your senses are heightened, making you feel more alive, more vibrant, more vital. Watching, feeling and listening to the sound of the water, you feel as though it is washing away any and all tensions, cares and thoughts, relaxing and renewing you, leaving you feeling peaceful and contented, yet also refreshed and re-energised. [Pause...]

You rest beside the pool, enjoying this peaceful little haven of fresh, crystal-clear, sparkling and dancing water, and allowing your feet to dry in the warm sunshine... [Pause...]

After some time of enjoying the ambience of the pool and the waterfall, you slip your socks and shoes back on...

[OPTIONAL:]
[You now notice that behind the waterfall is a shallow cave, which is accessible from the sides by a rocky path. If you want, you can walk behind the waterfall – enabling you to stretch your fingers out and let the cool cascading water run through them – and you can look through the curtain of water back down towards the valley, seeing dancing colours and lights... Or, if you prefer not to explore behind the waterfall, you can simply remain beside the pool a while longer, enjoying the peace, the freshness, and the playful water-droplets as they glint and flash in the sunlight... [Pause...]]

[ADDITIONAL/OPTIONAL:]
[After you have enjoyed the pool and waterfall to your satisfaction, [ALTERNATIVE: After you have rested a good while,] you notice that there are some rocky steps going up the bank to the left side of the waterfall, which continue on from the path that you had been walking along beside the river. You carefully climb up the steps – which are not too steep – to reach the grass on top of the rocky bank above the crystal pool. Here you can

sit beside the water (which you can now see comes from a higher stream, that winds its way down from the distant mountains you caught sight of earlier); and you can watch the water wash over the edge of the rocky overhang to cascade and splash down into the pool, which is now below you (although it doesn't look that far down). From your new vista, you can also follow the course of the river and the valley, back from where you started your walk and beyond, and you can just about follow the silver thread of the river way into the distance, as it flows and winds its way onwards towards the ocean... [Pause...]

You notice that the sun has dropped lower in the sky towards the distant ocean beyond the wide valley. It has turned a pale orange, colouring the sky and small clouds gold and pink towards the horizon. You get up from the grassy bank and carefully climb back down the rocky steps.]

~~~~~~

You realise it is getting late now, and it is time for you to start your journey back. The light around the crystal pool and the waterfall has turned to a pale orange, casting golden lights over the splashing water. You take a last look at the waterfall and the crystal-clear pool, breathing in the freshness, peace, beauty and energy of this special little haven. Then you start to make your way back along the path beside the small river, back towards the high grassy outcrop, and around it so that you can see the pastureland and the wide grassy valley spreading out before you again. The sun has now turned a deep orange, lighting up the whole sky with a glowing golden-orange light, as you retrace your earlier journey back along the pathway.

You enter the pastureland again beside the small river, steadily making your way back... [Pause...]

~~~~~~

[OPTIONAL:]
[As you continue back along the river path, you notice a graceful red deer grazing on your right side, not far from where you are walking. The deer looks up at you and gazes right at you from a few metres away – but doesn't seem frightened – and neither are you. As you come level with its position, the deer turns and begins slowly trotting in the same direction that you are walking, as though acting as a friendly guide to see you safely on your way home. You notice its slender powerful legs, its sleek shiny red-brown coat, its gentle, kindly face and wide intelligent eyes. Once the valley has widened out again, the deer halts briefly and seems to exchange glances with you once again, as though to bid

you farewell. It then turns towards the low hills to your right and trots off back into its own world again.]

~~~~~~

You now gradually allow the image of the pastureland to fade, along with the image of the riverside pathway, as you begin to bring your awareness back to the present – starting to become aware once again of your breathing… the sensation and rhythm of your breath… and starting to remember where you are, the room you are in.

You start to become aware once again of your body (sitting in the chair or lying on the floor)… So… start to take a couple of deeper breaths now, bringing your awareness back to your body (sitting or lying here in this room), preparing your body to start moving again soon. And once again, take a couple of deeper breaths, re-energising your body and mind. Start to become aware of your fingers and your toes, and start to stretch your fingers and wriggle your toes a little. Bring your awareness back fully to your body now… And, when you are ready, give yourself a good stretch. When you are ready, gently open your eyes… (If you are lying down, gently roll yourself onto your right side, before carefully and slowly sitting up…) And just sit for a few more moments to make sure you are fully grounded and back in the present.

Copyright © Amanda Jackson-Russell 2021

Copyright © Amanda Jackson-Russell 2021

Visualisation
– Temple of Healing in a Woodland Clearing –
(Including Healing for Self and Others)

Find yourself walking along a woodland pathway on a late spring day, the ground dusty, and rustling and crackling with small twigs and leaves. The trees are tall and elegant, forming a high canopy over your head, as the branches on either side meet above you and caress each other gently, and a soft breeze rustles their new leaves. The sun high overhead finds breaks between the leaves of the trees, sending thin shafts of light before you and forming dappled moving lights on the path. You walk easily, taking your time to notice the faint scents of the woods – mustiness from mosses growing around the trees, occasional scents of wild garlic, then the sudden sweet aroma of wild hyacinths. Bluebells and other delicate woodland flowers of yellow, blue, pink, white and scarlet appear here and there, pushing up between piles of dried leaves and twigs to the sides of the path. Small birds dart about in the undergrowth, and scuttle quickly away as you walk by. A pair of squirrels are playing tag in the branches of the trees, flicking their tails and jumping from branch to branch.

As you continue along the path, you notice ahead of you that there is brighter light, almost like the end of a tunnel. As you approach the light, you see that the trees thin out and come to an end for a moment, to reveal a lush, grassy clearing the the middle of the woods. To the left of you is a small, babbling stream, with crystal-clear water washing over rocks and pebbles, and tiny fishes darting here and there... The stream's presence adds to the freshness and peacefulness of the clearing…

The brilliant light of the sun is streaming down, lighting up this small clearing – a bright, light, warm, sunny glade in the middle of the woods – a woodland haven of light. The trees surrounding the clearing are reflecting the light off their fresh new pale-green leaves – reflecting bright green and golden light all around – filling this space… The trees and the grass and the light seem to create a sacred space – a natural temple of love and peace and healing.

Near the centre of the clearing is the stump of an old oak tree, its comfortable breadth providing you with the perfect place to sit in this healing temple of Nature. You make your way over to the old stump, sitting down, and lifting your face upwards towards the pale warm sun. You feel warm and safe, content and peaceful…

As you sit in the peace and the warmth, you instinctively feel a golden healing light beaming down on you... forming a sphere of light around you... surrounding you in its love and protection... and passing down through the top of your head... down your spine... spreading out through the whole of your body... Protecting, relaxing, nourishing and healing you…

You take a few deeper breaths, and let them go slowly... and feel the benevolent, healing energy relaxing you more and more… You allow the healing energies to work their magic on you... warming you... revitalising you... healing you... washing away all worries, cares, aches and pains, tensions... filling you with a wonderful feeling of restoration and renewal and new vitality...

You think about other people in your life... and others that you don't know... and other beings and life on this planet – maybe animals, pets, trees, distant countries, forests, the oceans... And you feel a desire to invite others to join you in this healing experience...

So... you take a few moments to think about and invite others into this healing space with you... People dear to you... Loved ones whom you want to experience healing... And other beings and life-forms... You welcome them all to join you in this sacred space... And you ask the Highest Source of Love, Light and Healing to send each and every one of you the help and healing that you each most need at this time, for your Highest Good, and the Highest Good everywhere...

Take all the time you and your companions need to absorb the love, light, peace, healing and renewal... Breathe it all in deeply, and let your breath go slowly... Feeling the healing transformation occurring... Allow it to happen... Welcome it... Give thanks for it... And send love and blessings to all those around you... And feel their love and blessings towards you... Feel the love and peace and connection... with the Earth and all its beings... with the Universe... with the Highest Source of Love and Light and Healing... Know that you and all beings are connected to this always... and that you can draw on its love and strength and wisdom and healing whenever you want or need to...

The sun is now starting to sink below the line of the tree-tops... The (light and) ambience is still warm and bright, but the trees are starting to cast shadows across the woodland clearing... The essence and spirits of those who have joined you here gradually start to disperse, nodding their love, respect and appreciation to you as they go... It is time now for you to start to make your way back...

You get up from the old tree stump, taking in one last image of the clearing and the babbling stream… The grass and trees are now reflecting a darker rich green... You make your way back across the soft grass to the opening in the trees where the woodland path is, and you follow it back. There is still enough pale golden light flickering and glinting between the leaves and branches of the trees for you to make your way back easily and safely...

And now, you gradually allow the image of the woodland and the path to fade, as you begin to bring your awareness back to the present – starting to become aware once again of your breathing, the sensation and rhythm of your breath, and starting to remember where you are, the room you are in. You start to become aware once again of your body (sitting in the chair or lying on the floor). Start to take a couple of deeper breaths now, bringing your awareness back to your body (sitting or lying here in this room), preparing your body to start moving again soon. And once again, take a couple of deeper breaths, re-energising your body and mind. Start to become aware of your fingers and your toes, and start to stretch your fingers and wriggle your toes a little. Bring your awareness back fully to your body and when you are ready, give yourself a good stretch. When you are ready, gently open your eyes. (If you are lying down, gently roll yourself onto your right side, before carefully and slowly sitting up.) And just sit for a few more moments to make sure you are fully grounded and back in the present.

(Developed from concepts arising during NFSH training and attendance at healing development groups, 1986–1990.)

Copyright © Amanda Jackson-Russell 2021

Copyright © Amanda Jackson-Russell 2021

Visualisation
– Moonlit Beach, White Horse and Magical Journey –

Imagine you are sitting in a beach-front conservatory on a summer's evening... cool and peaceful after the warmth of the day... the sun has set and, through the windows, you can see a full moon rising on the horizon over the sea... You step out from the conservatory, and down some shallow stone steps that lead down to the beach... You feel a soft cool breeze caressing your skin... it feels comforting and refreshing after the heat of the day...

Barefoot, you step softly through some sand dunes to the white sand of the moonlit beach... The deep indigo sea is reflecting the moonlight, which seems to form a rather enticing silver pathway over the waves... To the right, at that end of the beach are some tall white cliffs...

You approach the cliffs... a white horse is waiting... he whinnies softly... he seems to recognise you...

You climb up on some rocks and lift yourself up onto the horse's back, clasping your hands around thick strands of his mane and settling into his comfortable back... somehow, you feel totally safe, peaceful and somewhat excited... wondering what is going to take place...

Your white mount starts trotting along the edge of the seashore... the moon lighting your path... you look up at the full moon, casting its light over the waves... Then suddenly, the horse and you are up in the air... floating above the water... climbing higher... up and up... until you can see the whole moonlit expanse of the ocean... and millions of bright stars in the sky above... and the beach and cliffs behind you are receding into the distance... getting smaller and smaller...

You travel through the velvet air... through the indigo sky and sparkling stars... the water and waves glinting below in the moonlight... [Pause...]

After a while, you notice that, ahead of you, towards the horizon, the sky is becoming lighter... Dawn is just beginning to break... [Pause...]

Soon, you see an island ahead of you... soft golden sand, low green hills, palm trees, lush valleys with streams and gentle waterfalls...

Your mount starts to lower down towards the island beach... towards brilliant turquoise sea and waves… and gently alights on the beach... He lowers his front legs and head, allowing you to slide safely onto the soft white sand...

The whole beach... the turquoise sea... the green grassy banks... the palm trees... the sun and the sky... they all seem to exude an amazing atmosphere and energy of peace, vitality and wellbeing... The horse wanders over to a grassy bank beyond the beach, to lazily and contentedly graze... You walk barefoot along the beach in shallow crystal-clear water as gentle waves ebb and flow... You feel the warm silky water caressing your feet... You breathe in the freshness of the gentle breeze, catching the scents of ozone and salt in the air... Deeply inhaling the magical energy from all around... Feeling as though your whole body, mind and spirit are being revitalised... renewed... restored... [Pause...]

After a while, as the sun climbs higher in the sky and warms your face and whole body, you spot a palm tree a little way ahead up the beach... You make your way over through the fine gold-white sand and sit down to rest in the shade of the palm leaves... And you just allow yourself to drink in and absorb the sights, scents and sensations of this place... the turquoise of the sea... the bright blue of the sky... the white-gold of the sand... the freshness of the air... the green of the grassy banks behind the beach... Time just seems to drift... There is nothing to concern or worry you... You can just rest and relax completely...

[Long pause...]

After some time, you detect a gentle splashing sound that seems to come from some rocks a little way from where you are sitting... it is the gentle splashing of spring water as it cascades down from the hills, sparkling in the sun as it runs through a rocky course towards the sea... You stand up and walk over to the spring water, bending down to let its fresh coolness run through your fingers... and then, cupping your hands, you take a refreshing drink of the cool clear water... and splash some on your face and arms... [Pause...]

The sun has begun to sink a bit lower in the sky now... turning the sea a deeper rich turquoise-blue... and the sand a deeper golden yellow-orange...

Looking up, you see the white horse is now nearby and gently approaching you... He stops to take a drink from the spring water... You realise it's time to be going now... returning back to where you came from...

You climb up onto the rocks next to the horse and once again lift yourself up onto his back, settling down comfortably and burying your hands in his mane…

Soon you are both up in the air again… winging your way over the turquoise waves... you take one last look as the image of the magical island recedes into the distance behind you… [Pause...]

You are flying higher and higher... up and up... and the sky starts to turn a deep indigo-purple... bright stars are appearing in their thousands... and you see the moon... lighting your way... casting a long silvery pathway on the now black-velvet waters below you... as you follow it silently, smoothly and safely back… [Pause...]

At last... once again… you see ahead of you the white moonlit beach from where your adventure began... the light glinting off the waves along the shoreline... and the outline of the tall white cliffs to one end of the beach... You get closer and closer... and your horse companion begins to lower down towards the beach... finally alighting gently but firmly on the sand... Once again, he lowers his front legs and head, enabling you to slide safely onto the sandy moonlit beach by the white cliffs... You thank your companion, and softly stroke his nose and neck... He whinnies softly... and then turns and trots away into the night…

~~~~~~

[OPTIONAL:]
[You make your way back up the beach, through the sand dunes and back up the stone steps to the conservatory... Sitting back down again in a comfortable easy chair... and looking back out towards the beach and into the night sky...]

~~~~~~

The image of the moonlit beach starts to fade now... and you begin to return your awareness to the present day and time... Feeling as though you have had a wonderful magical healing dream – a journey to a special magical place – and feeling relaxed, peaceful and revitalised... and knowing that you can return again to that place another day...

Copyright © Amanda Jackson-Russell 2021

Guided Meditation/Visualisation
– Meeting and Connecting with Your Spirit Guides and Angels –

Before you begin this meditation, you may wish to have a pen and notebook close at hand, so that at the end, you can make notes of any messages and communications that you may receive.

[Grounding, Centring, Connecting (Attuning) and Protecting]

Sit comfortably in your chair. Have your eyes closed, with your feet flat on the floor. Have your spine straight, and your hands resting in your lap or on your thighs with the palms facing upwards. Focus on the gentle flow of your breath, breathing from your abdomen, and allowing your tummy to expand on the in-breath, and relax back again on the out-breath...

[Body-Scan Relaxation]
First, become aware of your physical body from your toes all the way up to the top of your head... Now, you are going to progressively rotate your awareness around your body... becoming aware of each part in turn...

Become aware of the area from your right foot to your knee... then your right knee to your hip... your left foot to your knee... then your left knee to your hip... Become aware of your right hand to your elbow... your right elbow to your shoulder... Then your left hand to your elbow... your left elbow to your shoulder...

Become aware of your right buttock... left buttock... the small of your back... the middle of your back... the upper back... Then the whole spine... from the base to the neck...

Become aware of the tops of your shoulders... the back of your neck... the back of your head... the top of your head... the forehead... right eyebrow... left eyebrow... right eye... left eye...

Then your right ear... left ear... nose... right cheek... left cheek... lips... chin... tongue... jaw... and throat... Then become aware of the front of the neck... the collar bones... the upper chest... the centre of the chest... the heart... solar plexus... abdomen... groin area... and lastly, the base of your spine...

Now focus your awareness on your feet... feel them very firmly on the floor (or ground)... Imagine strong branching roots extending down from your feet into the Earth, extending down and down... to the centre of the Earth... earthing and grounding you... Breathe in the Earth energy – strong, vital, nurturing, strengthening, grounding... Breathe this energy up through your feet, up your legs, through your knees... and thighs... and hips... Breath this energy into the base of your spine, the lower abdomen, the upper abdomen... up into the solar plexus... up into the heart... Be aware of the heart centre and breathing the Earth energy up to this point...

[Attuning to the Higher Realms/Spirit/Light]
Now become aware of the light of Spirit above your head... from the Highest Source of Love and Light and Wisdom and Healing... Connect with the light... bring it down through your crown chakra... down to your eyebrow chakra... into the centre of your head... Allow this Spiritual energy, love and light to flow down your neck... down your spine... into the throat chakra... into the heart chakra... (Feel the Spiritual and Earth energies mixing and mingling...) Allow the light to flow down into the solar plexus... the upper abdomen... the lower abdomen... the base chakra... [Pause...]

Then shoot this light energy down through your hips, legs and feet into the Earth... down into the centre of the Earth... grounding this Spiritual energy on the Earth plane...

Now bring your awareness back to your heart centre... breathe in and out of your heart centre... feel the connection between the highest source of light and your heart centre...

[Protection]
Feel the light in your heart centre... and breathe in and out of your heart centre... Now imagine the light in your heart centre expanding... expanding more and more... until you feel it totally surrounding you... encircling you... completely enclosing you in a shining sphere of golden and white light... in which you are totally safe and protected...

[Ask to Connect to Your Spirit Guides and Angels]
Now bring your awareness back to your heart centre... and the connection between your heart centre and the highest source of light...

Ask now to connect with your spirit guides and angels... And give permission to your guides and angels – those beings from the highest sources of love and light and healing and wisdom – to connect with you...

[Travelling Through Doors in Your Consciousness to Meet Your Spirit Guides and Angels]

Now take your awareness to your eyebrow centre... Visualise a door in your consciousness... Make the door as real as possible... Notice its features... its size, its shape, its texture, its colour, the handle or door knob... Now open the door and walk through the doorway, closing the door behind you...

Find yourself in a corridor... Walk down the corridor... You come to a staircase [or escalator or lift]... Find yourself going up and up and up... up and up... Soon you find yourself in another corridor... Walk down the corridor... Then there's another door... This is the door to your Hall of Learning... Open the door and walk through, closing it behind you...

Notice the features of the room... There may be bookcases, a table or desk, some comfortable chairs... A warm fire in the hearth... There may be an altar with candles, crystals, spiritual symbols, incense... Spend a little time here, absorbing the energies of learning, wisdom and knowledge...

At the far end of the room, there are some wooden double doors... You approach the back of the room and open the doors... going through them... and closing them behind you...

You find yourself in a beautiful garden, with lawns and flower borders... You walk around the garden... taking in the sights... the lawns, flowers, plants and trees... You feel the sun on your face... and notice the blue sky with small clouds dotted here and there... Feel the gentle breeze on your face... Notice the perfumes of the flowers... The rustling of the trees in the gentle breeze...

As you walk further down the garden, there is an arbor – like a hidden gateway and pathway – adorned with jasmine and honeysuckle... You walk through... and it leads you to an inner garden...

You see there's a fountain... You walk over and sit down on a bench by the fountain...

[Connecting with Your Spirit Guides and Angels]
You notice that, in a further corner of the garden, there's a summer house... The door to the summer house opens... And a figure or figures emerge from the summer house... They are your spirit guides or angels... They walk over to meet you... And sit down

beside you... They ask to connect with your heart centre... and you invite them to do so... You too focus on and connect with your heart centre...

You can ask them whether they are guides or angels or both... Wait for a response... [Pause...]

You can ask them for guidance... Ask them any question you wish... Listen and wait... [Pause...]

If you wish, you can ask your guides and/or angels if they have a message (or messages) for you... [Pause...]

You can ask them to give you whatever guidance you most need at this time... to enable you to heal from a particular issue... or to help you move forward in your life... Listen and wait... [Long pause...]

If you don't understand the message or are unclear about it, ask them to put it in such a way that it is Specific, Practical and Relevant... Listen and wait... [Long pause...]

When you have received their messages and guidance to your satisfaction... thank your guides and/or angels... and take a little time to absorb the meanings... [Pause...]

After a little while, your guides and/or angels withdraw...

[Return Journey Back to Everyday Consciousness]

Finally, when you are ready, you make your way back through the garden... [Pause...] And back through the wooden doors to your Hall of Learning... back out through the door at the other end of the room... along the corridor... back down the stairs [or down the escalator, or down in the lift]... down and down... until you are back at the first corridor...

You walk back along this corridor... back to the door in your consciousness... Notice its features again... Open the door and walk back through the doorway, closing the door firmly behind you...

Now become aware of your crown chakra, and bring the energy level down, closing the crown centre down to a safe level... do this with each of the chakras in turn... (If you like, visualise drawing a circle with a cross in it over each of the centres in turn)... the crown... the eyebrow centre... the throat centre... the heart centre... the solar plexus... the abdominal centre(s)... and finally the base of the spine...

[OPTIONAL: Once again, mentally thank your guides and/or angels for their loving communication and the messages they have given you...]

Become aware of your buttocks and hips in contact with the chair... become aware of your legs... your feet... your contact with the ground and the Earth... Feel well connected and grounded in your physical body and with the Earth... Become aware of your whole body now, from the top of your head to the tips of your toes...

[Protection]
And now imagine a great swirling cloak of deep blue-purple protective energy, like the midnight sky... and wrap this cloak around you so you are totally covered from head to foot... Make sure it is completely sealed above you and beneath you, as well as all around... totally enclosing you and protecting you... Imagine placing a symbolic cross over the front of your face to ensure complete protection...
[ALTERNATIVE TO THE ABOVE: Imagine placing a black obsidian pyramid around you, sealed to the front, sealed to the back, sealed to the left, sealed to the right, sealed to the top, sealed to the bottom... Filled with healing light and violet flame surrounding you to protect you and to reflect and transmute negativity... Silently say "Thank you, thank you, thank you..."]

[Returning to Everyday Consciousness]
Now start to return your awareness to the present day... Become aware of the room around you again... Become aware of your breathing again, and take a couple of deeper breaths now... Become aware of your fingers and toes... and give your fingers and toes a wriggle and a stretch... Place your hands palms downwards on your thighs to completely ground yourself.. [OPTIONAL: Rub your palms over your thighs, making contact with the physical again...] And finally, open your eyes...

(If you wish, take your pen and notebook, and write down any messages or guidance that you have received from your guides and/or angels... and any other related thoughts that occur to you that may help clarify the messages. In the coming days, you can re-read your notes and perhaps gain more insight into the words...)

Copyright © Amanda Jackson-Russell 2021

Goal Visualisation and Realisation
(Including New/Future Self-Image)

[Introduction and Initial Preparation]

[Introduction]
In a little while, you are going to relax very deeply and then visualise your goal or goals. You will then strengthen these images and visions. Then you are going to imagine, in detail, that you have achieved your goal. However, first of all, you need to do some preparation to enable you to visualise your goal in as much detail as possible. Your goal may be something outside of yourself – eg. a job, a place you want to live, a new career, a new skill, a new relationship, whatever... Or it may be a changed version of yourself – a slimmer you, a more confident you, a more positive you, a healthier you, or something else... Frequently the two things go together (ie. your goal(s) and a new self-image). Often, in order to achieve a particular goal, you may need to develop new qualities. Conversely, a new version of yourself will have repercussions on the people you find yourself with and the environments and activities you find yourself in. So when visualising and realising a goal or goals, it is often helpful to consider the person you will be as you approach and realise your goal – in other words, a new image of yourself – seeing yourself becoming the person who possesses all the qualities and skills, and taking all the steps, necessary to achieve your goal.

When setting and visualising a goal, it can also help if you can put a realistic date on when you would like to have comfortably achieved it and you have had a bit of time to adjust to it – for example, 3 months' time, or 6 months' time, or 12 months' time. If a goal seems too far in the future to motivate you or is perhaps going to take several long-term steps and stages to achieve, it may help to break down the overall goal into smaller more easily achievable (less daunting) sub-goals, and work on each of these in turn.

[Initial Goal Visualisation (Preparation)]
Before you start the main visualisation process, take a few minutes now to think about – and write down, if it helps – all the different aspects and stages (if applicable) to your goal. If you come up with several sub-goals, decide on the most important one to focus on for now (ie. the one you want or need to achieve first).

For a few moments, I'd like you to close your eyes, and imagine you have already achieved your goal. Imagine being in the situation where you have accomplished your goal, as if you are there right now. Imagine it in as much detail as possible.

~ Think of where you are and what is happening... [Pause...]
~ Imagine what you are feeling – what positive emotions do you now feel, having achieved your goal? [Pause...]
~ Imagine how your body feels – what positive sensations do you now feel? [Pause...]
~ Think about how you now act, behave and speak... [Pause...]
~ Think about what changes have taken place in your body language, your posture, your mannerisms, your facial expression, and your voice... [Pause...]
~ What positive thoughts now go through your mind about things? [Pause...]
About your life... your situation... your achievements... yourself...? [Pause...]
~ What other positive changes are you experiencing now? [Pause...]
~ Think about what social or material benefits might result from you having experienced all these changes and having achieved your goal... [Pause...]
~ Really experience having achieved your goal in as much detail and vividness as possible... [Pause...]
~ Really feel what it feels like to have achieved your goal... [Pause...]
~ Imagine smiling to yourself inside... [Pause...]
~ Feel a sense of pride, success, accomplishment, satisfaction, contentedness, self-esteem, confidence, aliveness, joy, wonder, and excitement about the future... [Pause...]

Now, if you would like to, open your eyes, take a pen and some paper, and write down as much as possible about the different aspects and details of how things will be when you have achieved your goal. Describe it to yourself in the present tense as though it has already occurred. Note down where you are, what's happening, what emotions you feel (how it really feels to have accomplished your goal), what bodily sensations you feel, how you act and speak, what you look like (your body language, mannerisms and facial expressions), what positive thoughts go through your mind, what social and material benefits may result from you having achieved your goal, and any other positive changes that happen or that you experience. [Pause...] Note down anything else that can make things even more real about the achievement of your goal... [Pause...]

[NOTE: *If you are listening to an audio recording of this script, pause the recording whilst you make whatever notes you need to. When you have finished, restart the audio.*]

When you've done this to your satisfaction for now, put your pen and paper aside (you can always change the details, if you want to, at a later time – and even the goal itself). Now, sit down in a comfortable chair... and prepare to relax very deeply and then carry out your visualisation and realisation of your goal... and the New You that achieves this goal... I will guide you through the process...

[Entering Deep Relaxation (Deep Relaxation Process)]

[Closing Your Eyes and Starting to Relax Your Whole Body]
Now, keeping your eyes closed, I'd like you to roll your eyes upwards behind your eyelids, and imagine you are looking upwards towards a point in the centre of your forehead. Keep looking upwards towards this point, behind closed eyes... As you keep doing this, the muscles of your eyes and around your eyes will start to tire... Keep looking upwards towards this point, behind closed eyelids, for as long as it remains comfortable to do so... Then when you really want to relax... just let your eyes relax and roll back down again to a comfortable position... [Pause...]

Good. Now, take a deep breath in... then, as you breathe out slowly, allow your eyes to relax completely... Let all the muscles of your eyes and around your eyes relax completely... as your whole body starts to relax... Relax your face completely... Let your whole body relax completely... Breathing naturally... Good... And now, for a moment, just imagine smiling to yourself inside... feeling good... relaxing deeper and deeper...

[Progressive Relaxation – Breath-Body-Mind]
Now, I'm now going to help you relax your body and mind a little more deeply. First of all, just be aware of your breathing again... Become aware of the flow of your breath and the gentle movements of breathing... [Pause...] Allow your tummy to expand gently with each in-breath, and relax back again on the out-breath... For a few moments, just rest your attention on this process of gentle breathing from the abdomen, allowing your breathing to settle into a slow, gentle, even rhythm... [Pause...]

And now, start to gradually make your out-breath a little longer and slower... [Pause...] The body naturally relaxes with the out-breath, so lengthening the out-breath helps the body to release tensions and relax more and more... [Pause...]

Now, take your awareness to the top of your head... Become aware of your scalp... your forehead... your eyes... your jaw, tongue and throat... Become aware of all the muscles of your head and face... [Pause...] And now, with each out-breath, allow all the muscles of your head, face and jaw to relax, release and let go... With each out-breath, feel as though you are breathing away any and all tension in your head and face... With each out-breath, allow everything to become heavy, soft and relaxed... [Pause...]

Now, become aware of your neck and shoulders... And with each out-breath, allow all the muscles of your neck and shoulders to relax, release and let go... With each out-breath, feel as though you are breathing away any and all tension in your neck and shoulders... Feel the tension draining away, flowing down your arms and out of your fingertips... With each out-breath, allow your neck, shoulders and arms to become more and more heavy, soft and relaxed... [Pause...]

Now, continue taking your awareness on down your body... releasing and relaxing more and more with each out-breath... Allow all the muscles of your back to soften, relax and let go, more and more... [Pause...] With each out-breath, imagine all the muscles in your chest are releasing and relaxing... Imagine your heart becoming more peaceful and relaxed... [Pause...]

With each out-breath, imagine all the muscles of your abdomen, and all the internal organs, are relaxing and releasing more and more... letting go of any and all tensions... [Pause...] And take your awareness on down through your pelvis, buttocks and hips... Feel as though they are sinking down and down... deeper and deeper into the chair... becoming heavy and relaxed... [Pause...]

And take your awareness on down now, through your thighs... your knees... all the way down your legs... With each out-breath, feel as though all the muscles and joints of your hips and legs are releasing and relaxing more and more... With each out-breath, imagine all tensions are releasing and letting go, flowing down your legs, down through your knees, through your calves and shins, through your ankles, and out of the soles of your feet and your toes... [Pause...]

And now, for a moment, become aware of the whole of your body, from the top of your head, all the way down through your trunk, to the tips of your toes... [Pause...]

And now, on the out-breath, imagine a huge wave of relaxation sweeping down your body from the top of your head to the tips of your toes, washing away any remaining tensions from your body... [Pause...]

And now, with the out-breath, imagine another huge wave of relaxation sweeping down your body, washing away any cares or worries from your mind... washing away any tensions from your nervous system... calming your mind and the whole of your nervous system... [Pause...]

And now, as you imagine another huge wave of relaxation sweeping down through your mind and your body, breathe away any negative feelings, emotions, thoughts, cares or worries... Feel them flowing out of your fingertips and your toes... flowing away and dissolving into nothingness... [Pause...]

With the out-breath, feel yourself releasing all cares, worries, fears, tensions... and any feelings of frustration, sadness, anger, guilt, resentment... anything that is no longer needed... let them just flow away on the out-breath... feel them washing away, flowing out of your fingertips and your toes, flowing away and dissolving into nothingness... [Pause...]

[Staircase to Relaxation]
Now, imagine that you are at the top of a beautiful white marble staircase. There are five steps down the staircase... And there's an elegant golden hand-rail to guide you down if you need it... And it's a very special staircase... because it leads down to a special place of relaxation...

In a moment, you are going to begin *slowly* stepping down the staircase... And with each step down you take, you are going to be doubling your level of relaxation... relaxing deeper and deeper. With each step down you take, allow yourself to relax even deeper again... much deeper again... two times deeper again... So, by the time you've reached the bottom of the staircase, you're as deeply relaxed as you can imagine being... So, picture the staircase in your mind now...

And beginning now... 5... Take a step down... Relax deeper... 4... Taking another step down... Relax deeper... 3... Taking another step down... Relax deeper... 2... And another step down... Relax deeper... 1... And down onto the last step... Relax deeper... Let go and relax completely... Pause for a moment here, and take a couple of slow relaxing breaths...

Now, in a moment (on the count of 0 [zero]), when you step down from the last step... imagine you are stepping down into a room or garden of relaxation... a place that feels so peaceful, so relaxing, so safe and comfortable, that you can let go and relax completely...

Beginning now... 0 [zero], stepping down into this peaceful, relaxing space... Relax deeper again... [Pause...] If you like, you can imagine the colours and features of this place, and perhaps rest on a comfortable couch or bench... Or you can simply allow yourself to drift in your imagination and just enjoy the feelings of deep relaxation... [Pause...] Feeling peaceful and contented... [Pause...]

And again, 0 [zero]... breathing in the peace and relaxation... [Pause...]
And again, 0 [zero]... breathing in comfort and wellbeing... [Pause...]
And again, 0 [zero]... letting go, and relaxing completely... [Long pause...]

[Goal Visualisation and New/Future Self-Image]

[Preparation]
Now, as you continue to relax and turn your attention inwards, you are focusing your attention on the goal you contemplated earlier, and getting ready to imagine, once again, what it would be like to have achieved those things... Focus on your desire to experience those changes, and let that desire grow stronger... [Pause...]

And as you continue to go deeper and deeper into relaxation, your imagination is growing stronger... and just as in a dream, images come easily and powerfully to you... [Pause...]

And now, begin to prepare to travel into the future, in your imagination... [Pause...]

[Future Progression by Counting Forward]
Now, in a moment, I'm going to begin counting from 1 up to 5... As I do so, you are going forward into the future, in your imagination, to a point in time where you have achieved your goal to your satisfaction... As I count, with each number, allow yourself to journey into the future in your imagination, towards the realisation of your goal... If you travel ahead of me as I count, just allow your imagination and the experience of your journey into the future to grow stronger and more vivid with each number...

So, beginning now.. 1... Starting your journey into the future in your imagination... 2... Travelling forwards in time... journeying towards the fulfilment of your dreams and goals... 3... Getting closer and closer... changing into your future self... becoming the person you want to be... 4... Nearly there...˙ imagining what is it like... feeling that it's happening right now... 5... Stepping right there, right now, into the point in time when you have achieved your goal... feeling what it's like to be this new person... living the life you want to live... Feel that it's happening right now... Picture yourself there... See the fulfilment and satisfaction of your goal(s) in vivid detail... Allow yourself to experience everything... It's happening right now... You know exactly what you are seeing and feeling and thinking... Notice how you are, where you are, what's happening... Notice how you now think, feel and act... [Long pause...]

[Contemplate Details of Having Achieved Your Goal]
You love the feeling of success... So spend some time right now, immersing yourself in the experience of having achieved your goal(s), seeing it in every detail... See yourself having accomplished your goal... Notice where you are, your surroundings... Notice what's happening around you... Notice what emotions you feel... Notice how your

body feels... What positive physical sensations you feel... Notice how you behave, how you act... Notice your body language, facial expressions, how you speak... Notice how you think, what positive thoughts now pass through your mind... Imagine what other good things are now happening for you... Imagine and think about the wider implications of having achieved your goal(s)... What possible social or material benefits now open up for you... Imagine and think about how your life now starts to improve more generally... How things just keep getting better and better... [Pause...]

[Reflect on Changes]
Just continue to visualise having achieved your goal, and think about what is now different about you and your life... What do you do differently now...? What's changed about the way you feel inside...? What things do you feel differently about...? How have your thoughts and attitudes changed...? How has your perspective on things changed...? What else has changed...? How do you know you have achieved your goal(s)...? What did you do to achieve your goal(s)...? How did you get to where you are right now...? [Pause...]

Think about what you have learned... What's the most important thing you have learned, now that you have achieved your goal(s)...? If you could talk to your past self, what advice would you give...? [Long pause...]

[Review Daily Routine]
Now, just take a few moments to go through your daily routine, and notice how you deal with things differently... Start at the beginning of the day and go through things at your own pace... Imagine what life is like, now you have achieved your goal(s)... Notice how your thoughts, feelings and actions have changed as you deal with things throughout the day... Notice what the main differences are compared with how you used to be... [Long pause...]

[Allow Visualisation Experiences to Sink Deeply into Your Subconscious Mind]
In a few moments, you are going to start to return once again to the present day... But before you do, know that the images and experiences of having achieved your goal(s) are now being stored deep inside you... And they grow stronger and stronger as your mind draws them deeper and deeper inside... And they become part of your self-image and sense of identity...

You love contemplating success... And you are inspired to meditate more and more deeply on the achievement of your goals in life... Your mind becomes more and more solution-focused... And you are now automatically drawn forward towards success...

It gets easier and easier for you to see yourself achieving your goals in life… to identify with that perspective… to see yourself as that kind of person… thinking, acting and feeling that way… And that creative process propels you forward to enable you to achieve your goals in life… [Long pause...]

[Return to Present-Day Awareness, Acknowledging and Honouring the Transformational Process]

[Return to Present-Day Awareness]

Now, in a few moments, you are going to return fully and completely to the present day, bringing back with you all those insights and positive feelings, into the here and now… Returning completely to the present day… In a moment, I'm going to begin counting from 1 up to 5… With each number I count, you are emerging from deep relaxation, with a sense of self-confidence, satisfaction and achievement emerging from within you and growing stronger and stronger… And you know with certainty [/for sure] that the seeds of a profound transformative creative process have been sown deep within you, and have already begun to grow steadily and powerfully… And you are now taking forward with you all the positive benefits of this process and the power of your creative mind… And, with each day that passes, you notice the effects of these positive experiences growing stronger and stronger… [Pause…]

So, beginning now… On the count of 1… Feeling strong and confident as you begin to emerge from this deep transformational experience… Feeling good… 2… Breathing a little more deeply… Your body feeling more alive and energised… 3… Your mind feeling strong and alert… A sense of confidence and wellbeing flowing through you… 4… Becoming aware once again of your surroundings, of the room around you, and the here and now… Your eyes feeling alert now, and ready to open… And on the count of 5… Opening your eyes now, returning completely to the present, and looking forward once again…

Copyright © Amanda Jackson-Russell 2013, 2021

Short Relaxation and Visualisation for Beginning a 1-to-1 Energy / Spiritual / Reiki Healing Session
(Including Script for Ending the Session)

[INFORMATION FOR THE PRACTITIONER/HEALER:]

This short relaxation and visualisation (or similar) is recommended for use by practitioners of energy/spiritual/Reiki healing as a prelude to the actual healing act, to help a client relax and enable them to enter a receptive mode that enhances the healing process. If the client is able to relax deeply and actively take part in the process, the effects can be greatly magnified.

Depending on your particular professional training or preferred mode of operating (and the client's permission/preference), you may be working on or off the client's body, ie. lightly touching the person or working off the body in their energy field/aura (or a combination of both).

Also, depending on available facilities, your particular training, and/or your preferred mode of operating (and/or the client's preference), the client may either be sitting in a chair or lying on a massage couch. However, this relaxation and visualisation works particularly well if the client is lying on a couch.

If the client is sitting in a chair, ideally the chair should have a straight back (to give good support to the client's spine) and no arms (so that the healer can easily access the client's arms and other parts of their body during the healing process). A shallow cushion or cushions – placed behind the small of the back and/or under the buttocks – can be used if desired. Also, if the client cannot comfortably rest their feet flat on the floor, a pillow or pillows can be placed under the feet for them to rest on. Have a light blanket available to partially cover the client if they desire it.

If the client is to lie on a massage couch, have a some shallow (not over-stuffed) pillows available. The client should ideally lie on their back and rest their head on one pillow (or possibly two). (Note: Their head should not be too high so as to cause excessive lengthening of the neck.) Another pillow can be placed under the client's knees if that is more comfortable for them. Have a light blanket available to cover the client (from the feet to the top of the chest) if they desire it.

Typically, if the client is lying on a couch, the healer will begin by sitting just behind the client's head. If the client is sitting in a chair, then the healer will begin by standing just behind them.

[SCRIPT FOR THE CLIENT:]

[Note: Instructions for the practitioner/healer are given in ***bold italic***.]

[Introductory Relaxation]
[CLIENT LYING ON A MASSAGE COUCH, WITH HEALER INITIALLY SEATED AT THEIR HEAD]
[Ask the client if they would like a pillow under their knees, and help place one there if that would be more comfortable for them. Make sure the client is warm enough; cover them with a blanket if they wish.]

[Say the following to them:] Make sure you are resting comfortably with your hands by your sides or resting on your tummy. Have your legs uncrossed with your feet flopping slightly out to the sides. Adjust your position if you need to. [Pause...] Now just allow your body to relax as much as possible...

[Rest your hands gently on the client's shoulders. Quietly say the following to them:]
Become aware of your head, resting heavily on the pillow... Become aware of your whole body, resting comfortably on the couch... Become aware of the whole of the back of your body... in contact with the couch... Become aware of your breathing... allowing it to become slow, gentle and even... And with each out-breath, feel your whole body sinking down and down, deeper and deeper into the couch... With each out-breath, feel your body resting more and more heavily... completely letting go... Allow the couch to take all the strain... nothing for you to hold on to... just letting go completely... sinking down and down... deeper and deeper... resting completely...

~~~~~~

[ALTERNATIVE: CLIENT SITTING IN A CHAIR, WITH HEALER INITIALLY STANDING BEHIND THEM]
[Make sure the client is comfortable. If desired/necessary, provide appropriate cushions behind their lower back and/or under their buttocks (making sure they are still able to sit upright) and pillows under their feet. Make sure the client is warm enough; partially cover them with a blanket if they wish.]

[Say the following to them:] Make sure you are sitting comfortably with your spine straight and hands resting on your thighs or in your lap. Have your legs uncrossed with your feet resting flat on the floor (or on the pillow(s)). Adjust your position if you need to. [Pause...] Then just allow your body to relax as much as possible...

[Place your hands gently on the client's shoulders. Quietly say the following to them:] Become aware of your whole body, resting comfortably in the chair... the chair-back supporting your spine... Become aware of the points of contact between your body and the chair...

Become aware of your breathing... allowing it to become slow, gentle and even...

And with each out-breath, feel your whole body sinking down and down, deeper and deeper into the chair... With each out-breath, feel your body relaxing more and more... your shoulders, arms and hands... resting deeply... Your legs and feet... resting deeply... Your whole body... sinking down and down... Feel yourself letting go completely... allowing the chair to take the strain... resting and relaxing more and more deeply...

~~~~~~

Now start to make your out-breath a little longer... Allowing your body and mind to relax even more deeply... [Pause...]

And now, with each out-breath, imagine you are breathing away all tensions, aches and pains, any discomforts... feeling them flowing down your body from your head, all the way down your body... down your arms to your fingertips... and down your legs to your toes...

With each out-breath, allow all tensions and discomforts to flow down your body and out of your fingertips and out of your toes...

And now, with each out-breath, imagine you are breathing away all cares, worries, thoughts, anxieties, upsets... feeling them flowing down your body from your head, all the way down your body... down your arms to your fingertips... and down your legs to your toes...

With each out-breath, allow all cares, worries and upsets to flow down your body and out of your fingertips and out of your toes...

And now, with the out-breath, feel a huge wave of relaxation and peace flowing down your whole body from the top of your head to the tips of your toes... [Pause...]

[Short Visualisation]

And now, in your mind, I'd like you to take yourself to another place... a relaxing place... maybe a place in Nature... any place you like where you feel comfortable, relaxed and peaceful... You can imagine yourself sitting in a beautiful flower garden on a sunny day... or on a beach... or by a river or lake... or on a mountain top... or anywhere you like...

Imagine yourself sitting in this comfortable, peaceful place... enjoying the views all around you... feeling the gentle warmth of the sun... perhaps a gentle breeze... the sights and sounds... (perhaps of birds... or of tree leaves rustling in the breeze...) Notice the colours around you... the scents and aromas... (of flowers, or fresh grass, or the fresh air, or the sea/ocean...) Notice the colour of the sky... notice the feel of the earth beneath your feet...

And just allow yourself to rest and relax completely... enjoying this relaxing place... breathing in the freshness and the peace... allowing it to restore, renew and revitalise you... [Pause...]

[Healing Session]

[Now proceed with your preferred/chosen energy/spiritual/Reiki healing session – whether hands-on, or hands-off, or a combination of both...]

~ ~ ~ ~ ~ ~ ~
~ ~ ~ ~ ~ ~ ~ ~ ~
~ ~ ~ ~ ~ ~ ~

[Ending the Session]

[End the healing session by returning to the head of the client (if they are lying down) or to behind the client (if they are sitting), closing down the energies (and ending over the crown of their head), and disconnecting your energy from the client's. Then gently place your hands on their shoulders again...]

[Quietly but firmly say the following to them:] It is time now, --------------- [say the first name of your client], to begin to bring your awareness back to the present... [OPTIONAL: bringing all those feelings of peace, rest and renewal back with you...] Become aware of your breathing again... the gentle flow of the breath... Start to

become aware of your body (lying on the couch OR sitting in the chair)… Become aware again of the room [or place] you are in… gently bringing your awareness back to the present time and place…

Become aware of the sensations of your body (lying on the couch OR sitting in the chair) … [Pause...] Bring your awareness to your fingers and your toes… and start to give them a little wriggle and a stretch… becoming aware of the sensations…

[Now gently remove your hands from the client's shoulders. Move back a little way from them and completely disconnect your and your client's energies…]

[Say to the client:] When you are ready, gently open your eyes… and give yourself a good stretch if you want to… bringing your awareness fully back to the present…

[Check the client is fully oriented in the here-and-now, and ask them if they feel okay.]

[IF THE CLIENT IS LYING ON A COUCH:]
[When they are ready, help them to sit up for a few moments on the couch; then help them safely off the couch.]

[IF THE CLIENT IS SITTING IN A CHAIR:]
[Allow them to sit for a few more moments with their eyes open, reorienting themselves. When they are ready, help them safely up out of the chair if appropriate/necessary.]

(Developed from concepts arising during NFSH training, circa 1986–1989, and volunteer work at Esher NFSH Healing Centre, Surrey, 1998–2000.)

Copyright © Amanda Jackson-Russell 2021

Group Meditation for Distant and World Healing

[GUIDANCE FOR THE GROUP LEADER:]

[Introduction]
This group meditation is best carried out sitting in straight-backed chairs, with the chairs arranged in a medium-to-large circle (if possible, place the chairs about 2 feet apart) depending on the number in the group. Have a small table placed in the middle of the circle with a white candle on it.

Allow everyone to get seated comfortably and settle down.

Ask someone to light the candle (or the group leader can do this).

Make a dedication whilst lighting the candle. You can ask for one from the group, or use a general dedication, such as "To all those who feel alone and in despair, and without hope – receive comfort", or anything similar that feels right in the moment.

[GUIDANCE FOR GROUP MEMBERS:]

[Group Meditation]
Sit comfortably in your chair, with your spine straight and supported. Rest your feet flat on the floor. Rest your hands comfortably in your lap.

For a few moments, rest your gaze on the light of the candle... Then gently close your eyes... and internalise the dedication message... If you wish, you can add your own dedication (silently) to the message...

Imagine the light of the candle before you, growing larger and larger, and brighter and brighter, until the whole room is filled with golden light – radiant, beautiful, loving... warming you... seeming to form a sacred temple of light all around you...

Become aware of your feet... placed firmly on the ground... and become aware of your body, resting down deeply in the chair... Feel your connection with the Earth below you... grounding you... If you like, imagine that there are roots emerging from the soles of your feet and extending down... deep down... into the Earth... grounding and stabilising you... keeping you safe... connecting you with the energies of the Earth...

Bring your awareness to your breathing, without altering it... Notice the rhythm of the in-breath and the out-breath...

Now, with each out-breath, feel as though all tensions are washing out of you through your feet... all worries, cares, physical aches and pains... feel them all flowing away, down and out through your feet... [Pause...]

And now imagine a glorious sphere of golden-white light just above the crown of your head... Its qualities are peaceful, loving and healing... And as you breathe in, imagine a shaft of this golden-white light passing down through the top of your head... Feel it flowing down the centre of your spine... breathe it in and feel it flowing through you... energising you...

Just breath in and out slowly and gently...

With each in-breath, breathe in this light... and take in love, light, peace and vitality... With each in-breath, receive strength, wisdom, understanding, cleansing... Feel yourself being replenished and restored... (charged and glowing with all the colours of the rainbow...) [Pause...]

Now feel this golden-white light flowing into and around your heart centre... And then begin to feel it flow out of you from your heart centre... and see it starting to form a circle of golden-white light around, between and among all the members of the group...

And now become aware of a loving, healing energy flowing between each member of the group... Feel this energy flowing to you from the person on your left, and feel it flowing from you to the person on your right... Feel the circle of love and light passing around the whole group, linking and uniting everyone...

Feel this circle of light widening and enveloping the whole group... blending and uniting with the candle light... and forming a shining sphere all around... enclosing the whole group here in an energy field of protection... warmth... love... peace... and healing energy... Feel it flowing through and among the group... and uniting everyone in its healing energy... a shining temple of healing light... [Pause...]

And now invite into this sphere of healing energy – this temple of light – all loved ones... and anyone – any organism – to whom you want to send healing... friends, family, work associates, neighbours, pets...

Invite them all into this sphere of healing energy… to receive whatever they need at this time, for their Highest Good and the Highest Good of All Concerned… to receive healing, comfort, peace, rest, relief from pain, relief from worries, grief, hurt, stress, loss, loneliness, hopelessness, health problems, negative states or living conditions or situations… [Pause…]

[OPTIONAL: Book of Distant Healing]
[If there is a list of names written in a notebook for distant healing, the group leader – or another member of the group – can read out the names, inviting all those people into the sphere of healing energy, to receive healing.] [You can say the following, or something similar: "And as I/we read out this list of names, we invite and welcome in all these people into this temple of healing, and pray that each will receive the help and healing that they need and is right for them at this time."*] [The reader then reads out the list of names slowly and clearly…]* [Pause…]]

And now allow yourself (each member of the group) to receive healing… in whatever way you need at this time, for your Highest Good and the Highest Good of All Concerned…

Feel this loving, healing, nurturing, warm, protective energy flowing through you, touching all parts of you… cleansing, clearing, healing, renewing, revitalising… transmuting and transforming any unwanted or unhelpful energies… releasing them out into the Universe… and replacing them with peace, joy, balance, harmony, love and light… [Pause…]

Now, feel this loving, healing, golden-white light again in your heart centre… As every member of the group starts to feel the same… the loving, healing, golden-white light in their heart centres…

And, as a group, begin to direct this beautiful healing energy out of your heart centres… out into your community… to all the people of your village, town or city… out to the whole of this country… and farther out into the wider world… beaming and spreading to all parts of the world… the Earth… Send this loving, healing energy out to all parts of the planet… directing it to anywhere you wish… everywhere… to touch every living being and organism on the planet… people of distant countries and continents… wildlife everywhere… to the trees and plants… to the animals, birds, bees, insects of every kind... to the oceans... and all the living creatures and organisms in the oceans... out into the sky and the atmosphere... cleansing and healing the air and planetary energies...

And see it going out beyond our planet... out into the Universe... a loving, peaceful, healing, beautiful, benevolent, powerful energy... spreading out and out... touching all planets, all star systems... all other beings from other worlds... out and out into the Universe... [Pause...]

And now... for a few precious moments... feel that love and healing being joyfully and gratefully and affectionately reflected back towards the Earth, and to all its beings and organisms, flora and fauna, animals and insects, plants and trees, the oceans, the lakes and river waters, the skies and the atmosphere... [Pause...]

Now start to bring your awareness back to your own energies... and your own body... Be aware once again of your heart centre, that is sending out these loving, healing, peaceful energies... And now begin to gently and compassionately lessen that beam of healing light going out into the world... not to completely stop it... but to just allow you to return safely to the present day and the physical realm... Allow all those loving, healing energies to continue to spread throughout the world and the Universe... but now begin to close up that channel from your heart... just to a safe level for you... allowing the healing energies to still project outwards from your heart as and when you feel happy and safe to do so... but also allowing your own energies to separate from that flow... to become reabsorbed back to you... surrounding you and keeping you safe and protected... Integrating back into your energy field...

Become aware again of you own breath – the inSpiration and the exSpiration – the words acknowledge the spiritual link to the breath – and bring your awareness increasingly back to your own physical body... Become aware once again of your physical body... in contact with the chair... becoming aware of bodily sensations again... Become aware again of your feet resting firmly on the floor (or ground)... And feel that deep connection once again with the Earth... and the Earth energies... grounding you... providing you with stability, safety, security... grounding you safely in the physical worldly realm... and providing you with the nurturing and vital energies of the Earth... [Pause...]

Connect deeply once again with the physical body... And bring your awareness back to the room (or environment) where you are sitting... Feel deeply connected with the Earth... But also recall and know your deep connection with Spirit... [Pause...]

Silently give thanks for all the beautiful healing that has taken place… Then bring your awareness fully back to your body… the present day… the present environment… [Pause…]

Take a couple of deeper breaths now… and let them go deeply and fully… Then start to give your fingers and toes a little wriggle and stretch… bringing your awareness fully back to the physical body… If you wish, give your whole body a good stretch… And when you are ready, open your eyes again… looking forwards… feeling renewed, refreshed and revitalised…

(Developed from concepts arising during NFSH training, 1986–1989, and volunteer work at Esher NFSH Healing Centre, Surrey, 1998–2000.)

Copyright © Amanda Jackson-Russell 2021

About the Author

Amanda Jackson-Russell is an energy healer, relaxation and meditation instructor, hypnotherapist, and freelance writer and editor. She originally trained as a medical scientist, qualifying with degrees in Physiology and Neuroscience. Amanda initially worked in medical research, then medical and health publishing. In parallel with her "mainstream" scientific and publishing work, she also followed her interests in natural and complementary medicine. Amanda holds a number of practitioner qualifications in areas including aromatherapy, hypnotherapy, emotional freedom techniques (EFT), massage therapy, Reiki, spiritual healing and yoga teaching.

www.Facebook.com/EnergessenceSolutions
www.ajrhypnotherapy.co.uk
www.inspiredpotential.co.uk

Other Books by Amanda Jackson-Russell

Jackson-Russell, A, PhD. *Laid Back Like A Labrador – Practices to Banish Anxiety & Stress.* Blurb, www.blurb.com , October 2020.

Essentials of Anatomy & Physiology Review Guides:
Jackson-Russell, A, PhD. *Essentials of Anatomy & Physiology – A Review Guide for Therapists, Yoga Teachers, Holistic Health Practitioners, Healers & Wellbeing Coaches.* Blurb, www.blurb.com :
Module 1: Cells & Tissues; The Skin; The Skeletal System, Parts I, II & III. November 2019.
Module 2: The Muscular System, Parts I & II; The Cardiovascular System, Parts I & II. January 2020.
Module 3: The Respiratory System; The Nervous System, Parts I, II & III. April 2020.
Module 4: The Endocrine System; The Digestive System. May 2021.

Jackson-Russell, A. *Spring Chakra Meditations – for Energy Clearing & Balancing. Spring Walking & Visual Chakra Meditations for Vitality, Harmony & Energy Healing.* Inspired Potential, April 2018.

www.ingramcontent.com/pod-product-compliance
Lightning Source LLC
LaVergne TN
LVHW081451060526
838201LV00050BA/1764